Reflection:
Principles and practices for healthcare professionals

Second edition

by Tony Ghaye and Sue Lillyman

QUAY
BOOKS
A division of MA Healthcare Ltd

Quay Books Division, MA Healthcare Ltd, St Jude's Church, Dulwich Road, London
SE24 0PB

British Library Cataloguing-in-Publication Data
A catalogue record is available for this book

© MA Healthcare Limited 2010
ISBN-10: 1 85642 391 3; ISBN-13: 978 1 85642 391 5

Printed by CLE, Huntingdon, Cambridgeshire

Contents

Contributors

Tony Ghaye Cert Ed, BEd (Hons), MA (Educ) PhD
Director, Reflective Learning, UK
I am currently the founder and Director of a not-for-profit, social enterprise called, Reflective Learning-UK (www.reflectivepractices.co.uk). We work around the world striving to improve lives and livelihoods through strengths-based approaches to enhancing well-being, quality of life and positive engagement. I have worked at eight universities in different countries and am a professor in Educare (the education of those in the helping and caring professions). I have a background in social, organisational and positive psychology, education and healthcare. Much of what I do is as a strengths-based, organisational strategist, across sectors, disciplines, with multi-national companies through to grassroots community-based organisations. I have reported to Government departments in the UK and Australia and presented numerous keynote lectures at international conferences. I have written 20 academic texts on enhancing performance through reflective learning and published 107 refereed papers and book chapters to various audiences. I am the founder and Editor-in-Chief of the peer reviewed journal, *Reflective Practice – International and Multi-disciplinary Perspectives* (Routledge Taylor & Francis). My research and development interests are in high performance, teamwork, organisational well-being and positive engagement through reflective practices.

Sue Lillyman MA, BSc (Nursing), RGN, RM, DPSN, PGCE (FAHE)
Senior Lecturer, University of Worcester
As a registered general nurse and midwife I had experience in various areas, including intensive care, gynaecology, care of the elderly, and rehabilitation and acute medicine prior to entering nurse education in 1989. I held posts as senior lecturer at the University of Central England and Faculty Head of Quality Assurance before taking three years out to do voluntary work in Peru with street children and medical clinics in the shanty towns of Lima and in remote communities on the Amazon River. On returning to the UK I took up a post at Birmingham City University as route director for the post-graduate certificate in case management of patients with long-term conditions and module leader for older adult pre-registration nursing. I am currently working at the University of Worcester. Specialist areas of interest include improvement of patient care through reflective practice, care of the elderly and those with long-term conditions and care of vulnerable adults. My research and publications are related to care of older adults, nursing people with long-term conditions and using reflection to enhance care and quality of life.

Acknowledgements

We would like to acknowledge all our colleagues, in many places and cultures, who have engaged in positive conversations with us about the power and potency of learning through reflection. We would particularly like to show our deep appreciation to Simona Marchi, Francesco Consoli, Ruggiera Sarcina, Massimo Tomassini, Elisa Cavicchiolo, Bruna Lucattini, Debora Giannini, Emma Ciceri, Antonella Barile, Galina Markova, Hari Alexandrov, Antoaneta Mateeva, Furio Bednarz, Shiphrah Mutungi, Tunji Olaopa, Funmi Amobi, Anita Melander-Wikman, Ulrika Bergmark, Catrine Kostenius, Karen Deeny, Sarah Lee, Dan Shaw, Gavin Chesterfield, Maureen Sydney, Dave Collins, Andrew Jeffrey, Vince Russel and Philip Chambers.

About the series

The series is comprised of five books, entitled:

- *Reflection: Principles and practices for healthcare professionals*
- *Effective Clinical Supervision: The role of reflection (2nd edition)*
- *Empowerment Through Reflection: The narratives of healthcare professionals*
- *Caring Moments: The discourse of reflective practice*
- *The Reflective Mentor*

The books are about and for the improvement of healthcare practice and policy development. We have tried to write them in such a way that a variety of healthcare professionals might find them readable, enjoyable and useful. Reflection, after all, is a generic quality that makes healthcare professionals the kind of people they are! We do, however, admit to a bias in that we have included quite a lot of nursing material. This is not to devalue or marginalise the work of any other kind of healthcare professional; it merely reflects some of our own interests, limitations and frailties. It also reflects those we have largely worked with and those who have been willing to share their work with us. Although we have not been able to illuminate all the books with examples from the perspective of every healthcare group, we hope we have been able to offer each one some ideas, inspiration and hope so that, through reflection, practice may become more knowable, manageable and satisfying.

In the series we argue that reflection has the potential to transform both who we are and what we are able to do for and with others in our healthcare worlds. Above all else, we have tried to avoid turning reflection into something that might just be seen as anecdotal and 'soft', or like a slavish following of cycles or spirals. We do not wish to convey learning through reflection as though it were akin to 'painting with numbers'. In other words, simply procedural. It is also about deep things like values and feelings. We attempt to steer clear of valuing reflection in its own right, so to speak. We attempt to avoid it being seen as self-indulgent navel-gazing — as only about feeling better after reflecting on problems where, perhaps, we judged ourselves harshly and as failing in some way. In this second edition we offer the reader a more strengths-based approach to reflective practice. We hope the series points to the content of reflection being important, as well as reflective processes being challenging and sometimes painful. Skilful facilitation, high quality mentoring and the necessity for good support networks is important here. The bottom line is that we believe that reflection on practice can generate really useful knowledge that can help us to make better, wiser and more justified decisions about quality, safety and efficiency.

This actionable knowledge is derived from the context in which the healthcare professional is working. This is made up of an understanding of the self as a practitioner and lifelong learner, an understanding of the context of the patient/ client relationship and the whole context in which care is given. It is knowledge derived from, and based on, professional practice (Durgahee, 1997).

All the books in the series tackle what we might call 'the knowledge question'. It is perhaps the most fundamental one of all, as we use knowledge every time we make a practice-related move. There is knowledge which guides what we do and which helps us to improve our work. There is other people's knowledge, and knowledge about and for practice which we develop for ourselves, in collaboration with others. The role of reflection is significant with regard to the latter. Without knowledge of different kinds we cannot claim to be competent. The series makes an important statement about the kinds of knowledge which we generate through reflection. In brief, it is knowledge which:

- is about and for the improvement of self, the team and the context of healthcare
- is without apology but not solely practical in kind
- is 'local' and related closely to the actual clinical work context of the practitioner
- is generated and owned by practitioners themselves
- is often built up collaboratively and openly and not just individually and privately
- can be used to question existing practice and therefore to aid the development of a 'critical' stance towards healthcare
- is useful or 'good enough' to enable us to make more sense of our thoughts and actions
- contributes to the development of an enquiring posture which is an important element in being able to claim that we are lifelong learners
- *and*, above all, is appreciative.

(Ghaye et al 2008)

In this second edition we devote a new chapter to the nature and usefulness of this kind of knowledge.

We have tried to emphasise that learning through reflection supports acting with care and integrity and acting safely. Of course, not all learning is fun. Everything we learn is not sweet-smelling and rosy-red. However, certain kinds of reflection, if undertaken in a properly supportive and yet extending manner, may serve to energise individuals and clinical teams, open up new possibilities for action and may, over time, lead to improvements in what we do.

Currently many healthcare professionals are being swamped with policies and guidelines for a National Health Service which delivers more cost-efficient, safer and even higher quality care to patients. This is an NHS with clear national standards for services and for treatments, with high quality healthcare delivered locally through clinical governance, self-regulation and a commitment by practitioners to lifelong, and more recently, to work-based learning. The health service in the UK is responding to the Darzi report (DoH 2008) *A High Quality Workforce, NHS next stage review* which emphasizes a quality-focused, patient-centred, clinically-driven, flexible workforce that values people. However, good intentions simply are not sufficient in practice any more and many professional bodies, including the Health Profession Council, place importance on continuing professional development that reflects the Darzi report. Intentions have to be properly and sensitively implemented, reviewed and possibly refocused over time. So how can this be done? What is clear to us is that a service that does not value learning from reflection-on-practice, and a Government that does not have this at the very heart of its policies, runs the risk of being accused of oversimplifying the process of developing a modern and dependable health service. It also runs the risk of misunderstanding, devaluing and distorting the capacity and commitment of healthcare professionals to deliver its wishes.

Throughout the series we try to avoid both glorifying reflection and celebrating it uncritically. We have tried to describe its different forms and the many ways it can be facilitated. We have endeavoured to support, with evidence, the kinds of claims being made for reflection as the catalyst for enhancing clinical competency, safe and accountable practice, professional self-confidence, self-regulation and the collective improvement of more considered and appropriate healthcare.

In this second edition of *Reflection: Principles and practices for healthcare professionals*, we have included a chapter which introduces a new kind of reflection which we have called appreciative reflection. We have described, explained and justified it. Another new chapter is included for all health professionals and identifies the use and value of reflection in their practice, in line with continuing professional practice requirements. The book retains the 12 principles set out in the first edition. These serve to identify something of the 'landscape of reflective practice'. Each one is illustrated and clearly positioned within the literature. This second edition acts as the introduction to the whole series and attempts to encourage the reader into the reflective mode. The 12 'principles of reflection' described in it, and which are revisited and illustrated in the following four books in the series, are:

1. Reflective practice is about you and your work.
2. Reflective practice is about learning from experience.
3. Reflective practice is about valuing what we do and why we do it.
4. Reflective practice is about learning how to account positively for ourselves and our work.
5. Reflective practice does not separate practice and theory.
6. Reflective practice can help us make sense of our thoughts and actions.
7. Reflective practice generates locally owned knowledge.
8. The reflective conversation is at the heart of the process of reflecting-on-practice.
9. Reflection emphasises the links between values and actions.
10. Reflection can improve practice.
11. Reflective practitioners develop themselves and their work systematically and rigorously.
12. Reflection involves respecting and working with evidence.

The second book in the series, *Effective Clinical Supervision: The role of reflection*, explores the dynamic relationships between those involved in clinical supervision. This book was re-written as a second edition in 2007 to reflect the current trends and requirements of the NHS and included a chapter on action learning sets and what an appreciative relationship might mean and feel like in this context. Reflective practices and clinical supervision are contextualised in relation to the Clinical Governance and effective Human Resource Management agendas.

The third book, *Empowerment Through Reflection: The narratives of healthcare professionals*, explores the links between reflection and empowerment. It is a book in two parts: the first contains four reflective accounts written by practitioners; the second looks again at these and, in doing so, examines the notions of power and reality. The book questions the claim that 'reflection is empowering'.

The fourth book, *Caring Moments: The discourse of reflective practice*, shows how reflective practices, of one kind or another, help us to make sense of those aspects or our work which we have called 'caring moments'. It is essentially a book of powerful stories and an examination of the way reflection can help us to learn from them.

Finally, in the fifth book, *The Reflective Mentor*, we take a considered look at what being a reflective healthcare professional actually means in practice. We illuminate this by exploring the different roles and responsibilities of a mentor. We review the meaning of mentorship and its origins before discussing how mentoring impacts on practice and development. The important influence of emotional and social intelligence are explored in relation to the mentoring process.

We hope that this series portrays the holistic view (Bleakley,1999) which we have of reflection. We do not celebrate it uncritically but we do feel it plays a fundamental role in effective and meaningful learning. Above all else, what we are saying is that reflective practice stands for a collection of intentions, processes and outcomes. It is also a contentious phrase; it means different things to different people. The one phrase holds together many views of the nature of reflection, how reflection might be facilitated and what impact it has, or might have, on healthcare practice and policy development. So, as you read through the series, please do not expect to find a neat and tidy definition of reflection, a recipe which makes you think: 'this is the way it is done', or a list of positive outcomes of reflection which you should not challenge, which are real, always well-supported with evidence and achievable by everyone who engages in reflection. Fundamentally, the series is about 'learning'. Reflection, as we portray it here, has a concern for learning — learning from lived and experienced clinical practice. Johns (1999, p.297) expresses this notion of concern eloquently:

> *Concern can be likened to a fragile flower being blown by the winds of reality. Concern needs to be nourished, but also the winds of reality have to be understood, otherwise they may diminish concern in the need for personal survival.*

When we portray reflection, we are not speaking about it as if it were a static, de-contextualised 'thing', but more as a set of inter-relationships and interactions involving conscious and intentional practitioners in technical, social, professional and political service acts-in-context. These acts involve changes — changes in our disposition towards what we do, how we live out our caring values in practice, and change in the contexts in which we work. All change, though, is not improvement. Reflection, however, is interested in achieving improvement. It may be a difficult, threatening, sometimes bewildering process. We certainly need a 'safe space' to at least give reflection a fair chance to deliver what it promises; namely to make a genuine contribution to a more empowered, emancipated and enlightened NHS workforce and more meaningful, socially just and satisfying workplaces.

References

Bleakley A (1999) From Reflective Practice to Holistic Reflexivity. *Studies in Higher Education* **24** (3): 315–30

Department of Health (2008) *A High Quality Workforce; NHS next stage review.* Department of Health, London.

Durgahee T (1997) Reflective Practice: Decoding ethical knowledge. *Nurs Ethics* **4**(3): 211–7

Ghaye T, Melander-Wikman A, Kisare M et al (2008) Participatory and appreciative action and reflection (PAAR)–democratizing reflective practices', *Reflective Practice* **9:**4, 361 - 97

Johns C (1999) Unravelling the dilemmas within everyday nursing practice. *Nurs Ethics* **6** (4): 287–98

NHS Executive (1999) *The NHS Performance Assessment Framework.* HSC 1999/078, Leeds

Introduction

Into the reflective mode: Breaching the stagnant moat

Scenario:

The context was a busy coronary care unit (CCU) in a large hospital. Decisions were being made about admitting a patient from accident and emergency into the unit. The patient needed CCU support. The following is part of a conversation between two nurses, Fiona and Sally. Fiona was one of the nurses on duty at the time of the incident, and in the centre of the action. Here, Sally is engaging Fiona in a reflective conversation (see *Chapter 6*) some time after the incident.

Sally: Do you want to tell me what happened the other day on the shift, Fiona, because I think you had a bit of a time of it didn't you?

Fiona: Yes… well. I was on a long day and I was on the late part of the long day with another nurse, and there was a thrombolysis call from casualty. So I went down to see the patient who was in Room 1 with the A and E consultant and one of the casualty doctors. I did a heart trace and the patient, at that time, wasn't coming up to the unit, so I went back to the unit on my own. We had one empty bed at the time. We had a very poorly patient in bed 2 who kept having cardiac arrest. He, in fact, had six in all. During one of these cardiac arrests, the patient I had seen down in casualty was wheeled into the middle of the unit during this emergency procedure. We had no prior notification of him coming. He hadn't, in fact, been seen by the SHO [senior house officer] who was on and this patient who was new to the unit needed quite a lot of care. I instructed the nurse to put the patient in a side ward because I was busy with the patient in bed 2 during the cardiac arrest. In fact, I was quite annoyed with the nurse, though it really wasn't her fault for bringing the patient up. After things had calmed down a little she helped me admit the patient, for about five minutes. I did apologise to her and said that I realised it wasn't her fault… that I would try to sort out who had been responsible for making the decision for the patient being admitted without us knowing.

Sally: So, do you know who authorised the patient to be brought from A and E?

Fiona: It's a bit of a grey area. It was either the consultant who was seeing the patient from A and E, or it was the manager in A and E who was on duty at the time…or it was the SHO who was on duty…over the phone. There are a few different stories and it's going to be, hopefully, sorted out…but nobody was claiming responsibility.

This little cameo of life in a CCU enables us to learn many things. For example, it allows us to establish an early link between reflection-on-practice and its important role in helping us to make safe and ethical clinical decisions (Johns, 1998). In the example above, all sorts of decisions are being made. If we do not reflect on such decisions, we will never learn from our experiences of making them. We may never know what makes a 'good' decision! We may, therefore, never improve our actions. The decisions we make tell us a great deal about the kind of healthcare professionals we are, think we are, or hope to be. They say something about what might be regarded as 'best' or 'right' for a patient, given the circumstances. They reveal what we know, or do not know, and what we feel about a clinical incident. They demonstrate how well we cope under pressure, how well we respond to conflicting demands and whether we can act in a safe and accountable manner.

We make decisions, consciously and unconsciously, all the time and these decisions have both intentional and unintentional consequences. As one problem is faced and resolved, so it gives rise to a new situation and new challenges. Arguably, in healthcare work the commitment is constantly to seek effective, meaningful and ethical patterns of response in busy, turbulent and often chaotic clinical situations. Clinical, managerial and professional decisions are also linked to the notion of choice. Choices pervade all of life in healthcare. Choices are influenced by the values and assumptions of various professional groups, bodies and agencies. The choices we make, both individually and collectively, contribute to that rather slippery concept of workplace 'culture'. Sometimes, of course, we have no choice. There is no option. There is but one kind of treatment, one care pathway, one prognosis, one thing to say, to avoid.

On many occasions, though, the difficulty is to choose from an array of possibilities, to have some degree of choice. In clinical practice, to choose from a number of alternatives after reflection and discussion means something very different from being coerced to make a particular choice or having to make one from limited possibilities.

We can be both a part of the decision-making process and excluded from it. Reflection on the dynamics and structures which either inhibit or encourage participation in decision-making gives us a deeper understanding of the influence of organisational cultures on the quality of care. Sometimes it is difficult to argue that the decisions we make are rational and that the decision-making process itself is an orderly one (Carnell 1999). This is particularly so during periods of rapid organisational change and service development as we see in the NHS. This is what Egan (1998) calls the 'shadow side' of decision making. The bare essentials of decision making are to do with information gathering, processing or making sense of the information, choice, implementation and finally (and hopefully) reflection, not only on the impact of the implementation of the decision, but on every stage of its formulation. Egan argues that information gathering is rarely ever straightforward. There are the problems of too much, of too little, or of inaccurate and even misleading information to cope with. All decisions are therefore at risk. Hence the need to reflect upon them. Clients' stories and accounts, for example, are not always complete. The information we have to hand may be partial and open to distortion. Processing the information and making some sense of it is also a complex business. Because of our values and biases we may only focus on bits and pieces of the information available. We might miss the whole picture. Sometimes healthcare professionals and their clients might not make decisions based on evidence but upon personal preference, taste and such attitudes as: 'Well, I've done it like this many times before so I'll do it like this again.' Reflecting on the evidential base of our clinical decisions is very important. A host of things can happen at the point of choice and implementation. Interestingly, there are even occasions when we decide on one thing and then do another (more about this in *Chapter 7*).

Emotions, selective perception, uncertainty, organisational 'politics', different and multiple agendas, pressures of time and not always having all the information we need 'to hand', for example, all contribute to this shadow side of clinical decision making. Reflection-on-practice therefore plays a central role in effective clinical decision making. From the example above, with Fiona and Sally, we also learn that decisions are not simply discrete things but rather are part of a 'stream of decisions', connected directly or indirectly and framed within a 'system'. In other words, decisions made in one part of the 'system' (in accident and emergency, in our example) impact on decisions made in another part (in coronary care in our example). Making sound, sensitive and defensible decisions means that healthcare professionals, at every level of the 'system', need to engage routinely in conscious, systematic and public reflection-based practice. This can take many forms as we shall see in this book. Two Government publications (DoH 1997, 1998) as well as the increasing emphasis on clinical and cost efficiency and effectiveness, evidence-based healthcare and clinical governance (McSherry and Haddock, 1999), seem to suggest that now, perhaps more than ever before, we need to understand, own and live out the principles and practices of what it means to be rightly called a reflective practitioner, to be part of a reflective team and a reflective organisation. For many there is still a long way to go to find the time and commitment to work towards this. However, the context has now been provided for us not only to use reflective practices to work constructively towards contributing to the Government's results and league table-driven agendas, but also to use reflection to challenge and critique these very agendas. In this way, reflection helps to make our hopes, fears, intentions and expectations explicit. It is a way of communicating our practical knowledge of 'what it's like to work here'. It is how we communicate the perceptions we have of ourselves and our caring work. Reflection helps us to articulate the principled and practical support we need to achieve our personal and collective professional commitments.

In this book we try to set out some of the principles and practices of reflection-on-practice. In a sense, this book (and others in the series) are, of necessity, partial and one-sided. We do not address in any sustained way the complexities and subtleties of reflection-in-action. That is something for another series. This is not just another 'how to do it book'. It is not a techniques book because we do not wish to give the impression either that reflective practice is a singular thing or that it can be reduced to mere methods. Reflective practices and the development of the reflective practitioner have a history and a set of guiding values which contribute both to their identity and to their impact on care. It is more than methods; it is a whole disposition and attitude towards caring work. We have learnt that many of our healthcare colleagues have some difficulty with the term 'reflective practices'. Therefore, throughout the book, we use the more familiar term 'reflective practice', and we use it in its generic sense unless otherwise explained.

> *We should reject the certainty of any one meaning implied by the single term reflective practice.*
> (Newman 1999: 158)

This book also serves a second purpose. It is the first in a series of texts examining and illustrating the various ways in which reflection is used and the claims being made for its continued use. For example, one of the books focuses its attention on what we have called 'caring moments'. Here reflection is used to help us make sense of practice and to move our thinking and practice forward. Another book constructs the argument that reflective practice is at the very heart of that process currently called clinical supervision. A further book, for example, takes a close look at the claim that, through reflection, we can become more empowered in some way. Getting into the reflective mode always causes ripples, and the full extent of these cannot always be foreseen. You may feel uncomfortable when you read parts of this book. In some ways you might perceive it as being quite threatening because it invites you to address and resolve some potentially difficult personal, professional and organisational issues. For some, reflection-on-practice is either too painful or too threatening. For others, reflection is 'something we do all the time'. There may be those who feel that they are already sufficiently aware. There are others who may feel that such awareness of self, and self-in-context, is not particularly useful. Reflection is a process which can evoke deep emotion. We need to know about and be ready for this. Reflective practice is not simply about self-study, self-development and regeneration. There are also more 'militant' and critical forms which take account of the social, political and historical forces serving to constrain or liberate us in our work. Through this book we hope to foster a spirit of 'positive uncertainty'. Paradoxically this means using reflective practice to enable us to be positive (comfortable, competent and confident) in the face of uncertainty (ambiguity, doubt, fuzziness) as we work within a changing healthcare system. It is about feeling uncertain about the future, and positive about the uncertainty. Reflective practice provides a space for us to develop a positive attitude towards this uncertainty. Additionally:

> *The reflective practitioner makes a space. And while that space gives no guarantees, it allows us to think again, to do again, and slowly, to breach the stagnant moat between what most of us do and what most of us know we should do.*

(Anzul and Ely 1988: 27)

References

Anzul M, Ely M (1988) Halls of Mirrors: The Introduction of the Reflective Mode. *Language Arts* **65** (7): 20–7

Carnell C (1999) *Managing Change in Organisations*. Prentice Hall, London

Department of Health (1997) *The New NHS: Modern, Dependable*. HMSO, London

Department of Health (1998) *A First Class Service: Quality in the New NHS*. HMSO, London

Egan G (1998) *The Skilled Helper: A problem-management approach to helping*. Brooks/ Cole Publishing Company, Pacific Grove, CA

Johns C (1998) Unravelling the ethics of a good decision. *Nurs Critical Care* **3** (6): 281–2

McSherry R, Haddock J (1999) Evidence-based health care; its place within clinical governance. *Br J Nurs* **8** (2): 113–7

Newman S (1999) Constructing and Critiquing Reflective Practice. *Educ Action Res J* **7** (1): 145–61

CHAPTER I

An appreciative kind of reflective practice: From deficits to strengths

In this section we wish to set out some reasons for developing, supporting and experiencing the benefits of a new kind of reflective practice that we will call 'appreciative reflection' (Marchi and Ghaye 2010). This begins with an understanding of the power of the positive question. Before we explain this, we describe some of the major shifts in the practices of reflection in recent years. They represent some of the antecedents for our suggestion that, more than ever before, we need a new and better kind of reflective practice. One that is more appreciative in intent.

In the Foreword to a publication by Stavros and Torres (2006), David Cooperrider, one of the people who began the appreciative inquiry movement, wrote the following.

> *Put most simply: relationships come alive where there is an appreciative eye, where people are able to see the best in one another and create new visions together, with the desire for building not just new worlds but better worlds. (p. 15).*

In the time between the first publication of this book, and its second edition, there have been many shifts in the practices of reflection. Arguably one of the most significant is the shift from a pre-occupation with 'problems' towards a more explicit acknowledgement of the role reflective practices can play in improving what we do by focusing on strengths. Here are eight major shifts that will be discussed in further detail.

From 'I' to 'us'

There is still a widespread view of reflective practices as something done by oneself, usually alone and involving private conversations with one's 'inner voice'. It involves who we are and what we are doing. Also, sometimes, what we stand for. This is a conventional and still worthwhile view of reflective practices, which is often called self-reflection. It celebrates the centrality of the 'living I' and is visible in questions such as, 'What did I do?', 'How successful was I?', 'What do I need to work on to improve next time?' It is a kind of reflection done inside people's heads. Part of this book's expansion and fresh conceptualization of reflective practices is to make the point that:

- There are limits to learning alone.
- That more and different things can be learned when reflection on performance is done with others.
- That both individual and multi-disciplinary team-based reflection is an opportunity where clinicians and managers can demonstrate their caring about what they do.
- That individual, team and organizational reflection can be viewed as emotional labour.
- That a powerful site for learning is not just inside the clinician's head, but learning that arises from the wider social and organizational context in which healthcare takes place.

From cycles to questions

In many books about reflective practices, the way it is 'done' is often associated with reflective cycles or spirals. The conventional reflective learning cycle, is often associated with those proposed by Gibbs, Kolb and so on. A critique of cycles (and spirals) is offered in Ghaye and Lillyman (2006) in *Learning Journals and Critical Incidents*. In this book we alert the reader to the dangers of proceduralizing reflection and reducing it to checklists and recipes, of one kind or another. That the practice of cyclical reflection can quickly become akin to 'painting by numbers'. We also alert the reader to the danger of thinking about reflective practices as synonymous with writing about clinical encounters, as if thinking about them (after the event) and recording them, is all that is involved in reflection! We open up the notion that reflection on practice is necessarily contextualized and embodied.

A major shift in thinking and practice over the last eight years has been the shift from a preoccupation with cycles of reflection to one of the importance of asking questions. Here we make a fundamental distinction between deficit-based questions (e.g. What went wrong, why and so what do we need to get rid of?) to strengths-based ones (e.g. What was successful, why and what do we need to do to repeat and amplify this?). Central too is an understanding of the notion of the 'power of the positive question'. We offer examples of this later in this section.

From might do, to must do (bringing reflection into action)

In trying to improve practice we suggest we have to make an important decision about where to begin the process. In making these decisions, we need to think about if we should tackle our 'problems' first, or try to understand our strengths and successes. Not everyone agrees that paying attention to strengths and successes, rather than problems and failures, is the best way to start. The reason why we are advocating this is that it is the successes that need to be replicated and amplified, not failures and mistakes. This is a strategic issue of focus, emphasis and balance in professional development. Associated with this is the importance and the language of the positive. From other disciplines we know how important positive cognition and the processes of positive affirmation are to people. We know how affirmative affective states (e.g. like optimism, self-belief) are linked with mental, emotional and physical well-being. We know how appreciative coaching, high organizational morale, a capacity for co-operation, a sense of team cohesion and confidence in a positive (high achieving) future, are all things we must have and must do. So in this section of the second edition we take reflective practices into the arena of questioning their use merely to solve problems. We question the extent to which this automatically leads to better clinical and managerial work . In doing so we are also saying that healthcare organizations are not merely problems to be solved but are continuously in need of diagnosis, problem analysis and prioritized treatments.

From talking about, to evidencing reflection

Another major shift is that reflective practices, if done well, can help individuals, teams and whole organizations to transform experience into better and more actionable knowledge. In achieving this they help those involved to make better sense of their healthcare experiences in situations that are often complex, unpredictable, fast moving and pressurised. From this basic premise, we suggest that the process of framing and re-framing experience is important. This is linked with three essential components of working safely and with care and integrity. They are our sense of identity (e.g. as a nurse, AHP, doctor, manager, etc), the way we characterise others (e.g. as close colleagues, role models, people to avoid, be respected) and issues of power (e.g. to change, to improve, to influence routines, policy, to threaten, exclude).

A major shift has also been in the different ways the transformation of experiences, the (re)framing of them so that new and better options and alternatives become more visible and what might count as 'better' knowledge, can be evidenced and shown to others. It is a shift from talking about the way reflection has helped (or hindered) professional work, to a 'show me' position. This means that we are able to actually show evidence that reflective practices, of one kind or another, have made some noticeable improvement. This might be improvements in terms of;

- Feeling better about ourselves
- Being able to think in new and better ways about what we do
- Actually acting in better ways towards patients, carers and/or colleagues
- Positively changing the places where we work.

What counts as evidence of learning and how this is documented (e.g. in reflective portfolios) for accreditation, is a major shift.

From independence to inter-dependence of practice improvement and the 'workplace'

Traditionally, change and practice improvement were seen as a matter of human agency. In other words, if you wanted to change or improve something, you thought about it and then did it yourself, with the power and resources available to you. More recently, increasing attention has been placed upon the organizational culture/s in which clinicians and those responsible for healthcare management are situated. If 'culture' is defined as 'the way things are done here', then it can liberate or constrain, support creativity or stifle it. A shift has been to learn through reflection, in the workplace. This shifts our attention onto the inter-dependence between supportive and learning enriched clinical settings and practice that is safe and of high quality. The importance of reflecting upon the influence of context is shown in *Figure 1.1*. This also points up the importance of clinical leadership in promoting quality activity in the workplace.

Some evidence found in Øvretveit's review suggests that all the arrows

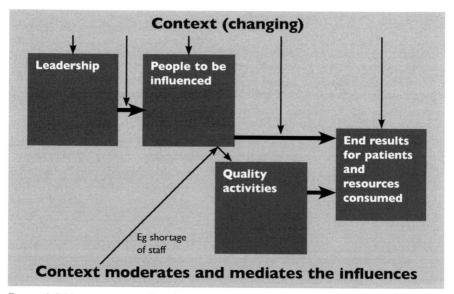

Figure 1.1 How context influences the nature and quality of workplace activity
Source: Øvretveit (2009) p. x.

are two-way. For example the leader influences, but is also influenced by all the areas indicated. In *Figure 1.1*, 'Quality activities' includes specific, short-term improvement projects, as well as people creating and running new and relatively permanent initiatives for improvement, such as promoting new structures, procedures and systems.

From learning for now to lifelong learning

The global trend for developing and sustaining opportunities for lifelong learning means that we now need to think carefully about how those in healthcare and its management reflect upon and contemplate future possibilities, and how those possibilities might be achieved. In doing this reflective practice/s play a pivotal role in identifying and securing effective learning opportunities throughout people's working life. The notion of 'productive reflection' (Boud et al 2006) emphasizes the importance of developing attitudes, knowledge and skills that support lifelong learning. This means reflection;

- With an organizational, rather than an individual intent, and a collective (team) rather than only an individual orientation.
- Reflection necessarily contextualized within workplace cultures and

thereby connecting culture with learning and performance.
- Reflection involving multiple stakeholders.
- Reflection that has a generative (generating possibilities and alternatives) rather than an instrumental focus.
- Reflection that has a developmental character.

From work-focused to work-based learning

Much has been written recently (Raelin 2008) about the increasing need to make the 'workplace', (rather than just the classroom, lecture theatre or laboratory), the natural and stimulating place to learn. We are mindful of this and acknowledge the need to foster and sustain learning enriched workplaces that enhance clinical care and management. This means knowledge creation and utilization as a collective activity, wherein learning for better work and management becomes everyone's business and where all relevant stakeholders demonstrate a learning-to-learn attitude, which frees them to constructively question underlying assumptions about meeting targets, providing quality care and managing in a cost-cutting (or efficiency saving) way. Organizational restructuring, new work arrangements, and training programmes will be insufficient unless the everyday activities and learning required to understand and enact these changes, are promoted and sustained. We suggest that effective practice/s play a crucial role in enabling this.

From changing practice to improvements in quality

When the term reflection has been used in the past, it has customarily been associated with changing individual practice. With the rise of team working (Ghaye 2005) there has been a shift of attention towards scaling up reflective practices beyond that to which one individual can expect to aspire and manage. By 'going to scale', more than change is possible. Stepping back, which is a fundamental aspect of reflection, and on a collective scale, brings with it the promise for real and sustained improvements in quality. Time and commitment to reflection can be the platform for quality improvement and the motivation for it. Ling et al (2008) see the connections between reflection and quality improvement like this.

Quality improvement involves stepping back from the immediate challenge of delivering care to reflect on the benefits of alternative ways of delivering care and, where appropriate, changing how care is delivered. It will often include an element of 'learning by doing' but should always involve an assessment of the resources required and the improvements in quality achieved. It is therefore not just another word for 'doing a better job' or 'working harder'. It is not always (or even often) 'whole system reform' but it does involve improving the design of at least one part of the system through which healthcare is delivered. (p. 2)

Appreciating the best of what is

It is healthy to question practice (our own and that of others) and the organizational contexts in which it is embedded. The challenge is, 'What do we begin to question first, how and is it safe to do so?' The natural default position for many clinicians and managers is that the practice of reflection is to concern itself with problems. That is problem finding and solving. The assumption is that this is the way to improve what we do, with and for others. The early work of Dewey, Schön, and the later works of Brookfield and Mezirow for example, all focus attention on various conceptions of 'a problem'. In this section we want to shift attention away from a view that reflective practice/s should be concerned with problems, and that this is both right and proper. Right because problems need fixing, attending to and getting rid of; proper because this is a way of demonstrating that we are attending to patient safety, being good at our job and using tax payers' money prudently. We wish to move way from reflective practices as a solution, looking for a problem. For some in healthcare, this is a frame-shift of some magnitude. We are going to suggest that we need to move towards a greater consideration of the benefits that might accrue from reflection upon strengths. What we are suggesting is that this would support the necessity for both depth and strength of self-belief needed by those in healthcare; would support clinician's ability to think positively, even when under pressure; and would support keeping one's inner voice positive. These are critical elements of a more appreciative form of reflective practice; a form that invites clinicians and managers to attend to the positive dynamics in their relationships with others. To attend to fundamental questions of the kind:

- What is currently working well?
- What is right?
- What do I see as the very best in the people I work with?
- What breathes life into good working relationships?

Appreciative reflection is fuelled by positive questions. Cooperrider (2001) suggests that using positive questions makes the following possible:

- *They release new positive vocabularies:* Positive questions re-focus individual and work group's attention away from problems and towards possibilities. By asking positive questions, we invite staff to use words, phrases, sentences and ideas that typically remain uncelebrated or underused in much of what constitutes normal organizational conversation.
- *They affirm variety of experience and encourage full voice*: If we adopt a social constructionist view, then it follows that language provides the means through which we communicate the sense we make of our worlds. The language we have available to us, to an extent, determines our possibilities for action. Positive vocabularies give us a chance of acting in the world, positively.
- *They help us value others:* Asking positive questions enables us to appreciate what others value and cherish in their work and so, understandably, what they want more, not less, of.
- *They foster relational connections:* Asking a positive question invites healthcare workers to reflect upon their practice and to think of something significant to them. What can emerge from this are expressions of our core values and commitments. They are essential things that connect us with others, and especially with patients.
- *They help build a sense of community:* 'By inviting participants to inquire deeply into the best and most valued aspects of one another's life and work, it immediately creates a context of empathy, care and mutual affirmation' (Cooperrider 2001: 31).
- *They can generate social innovation:* Appreciative approaches to work and working life (Cooperrider and Srivastva 1987), of which the positive question is a central feature, 'are based on the constructionist notion that organizations grow and evolve in the direction of their most positive guiding images of the future'.

When we inquire into our weaknesses and deficiencies, we gain an expert knowledge of what is 'wrong' with our organizations, and we may even become proficient problem-solvers, but we do not strengthen our collective capacity to imagine and to build a better future' (Cooperrider 2001: 34). To ask positive questions, we have to act with appreciative intent. If we can act with this in mind, we have a chance that it will lead to appreciative action. Our basic premise is that if we change the question we ask ourselves, we change the conversation. Change this and we have a chance to change the action.

Four kinds of appreciative intent

In this new form of appreciative reflection that we are advocating, four basic kinds of appreciative intent are required. They are;

1. *An appreciative intent towards knowing*: This is about, for example, recognizing our own gifts and the talents of others, focusing on what is and can be, rather than what isn't and can't be, what is understood rather than what is not. It is about being selectively attentive to the positive and essential.
2. *An appreciative intent towards relating:* This is about the active process of valuing and affirming the worth of others through interaction (e.g. good team working, mentoring) and dialogue. It is about caring about growth-promoting and healthcare performance-enhancing relationships.
3. *An appreciative intent towards action:* Here we suggest that appreciative action is inspired action. It is inspired by the positive intention for the betterment of self, team and organization; inspired by the healthcare professional's ethic of care; and inspired by organizational structures and processes that empower all involved to reach toward their highest potential.
4. *An appreciative intent towards organizing:* This is about organizing for the best individual, team and organizational performance, from an appreciative stance. It includes some frame-breaking propositions such as a commitment to trust building amongst multi-disciplinary teams; getting ideas to improve practice from everywhere; readiness for innovation; becoming emotionally intelligent; and developing learning-enriched clinical areas.

We suggest that acting with appreciative intent is an extension of the Lewinian premise that human performance/clinical action is critically dependent on the world as perceived, rather than the world as it is. We are putting the case forward that these four basic intentions are powerful reality-producing intentions. That they are promising practices for the co-creation of new, better and even more value-based clinical practice and learning-enriched organizational cultures. A key point we wish to make is that appreciative reflection is not simply a synonym for admiration or self-indulgence. We feel it represents the creation of new values and new ways of seeing things through the very act of valuing.

Avoiding the deficit trap

As we have suggested earlier, many of the practices in the general field of reflection are about individuals examining their own work, so that they are more able to change what they do in a particular context. This is very much in line with the early work of Schön (1983), who celebrated the ability and motivation of individuals to understand themselves better and improve themselves and their work. He said that we needed practical knowledge to achieve this. In Schön (1991) we read that what practitioners looked at in their working life was framed as 'puzzling' or 'strange'. This is still evident today in much healthcare work. A customary starting point for reflective practice is that which we might refer to as a 'problem'. In the work of Dewey (1933) we read that reflective practitioners learn by noticing and framing 'problems of interest'. Loughran (2006) looked again at Dewey's notion of a 'problem'. He suggested that although reflecting on problems is important, it should not be done at the expense of other aspects of our working lives. Loughran went on to state that if we use the word 'problem' we can easily get caught up with its negative connotations because it is so easily linked in our minds with words such as 'mistakes' and 'errors of judgement'.

We also suggest that focusing on deficits (only) is a powerful aspect of oppression. In working life we may be able to find the strength and strategies to combat those things we think oppress us. But if the real obstacle to improving what we do, in particular workplaces, lies buried within us, we can fight all we want, but it is likely to be to no avail. We are putting our physical, mental, emotional and even spiritual effort into the wrong things. A 'problem' in our healthcare work or working life is not simply a problem 'out there'. It can also be something we carry internally. The deficit trap is not just a question of what we do (or do not do). It is also a question of how we feel and think. A question of mindset. So instead of simply believing that the root causes of deficit-based actions is something about organizational cultures, it is possible the causes might be inherently part of us. One way of beginning to address this is to try to 'externalize' those things we internalize. To express them to others, perhaps through supportive reflective conversations; to write about them, perhaps in a journal or reflective log; or to inquire into them through some kind of work-based task or improvement project. Kaufka (2009) offers some useful starting questions. For example;

- What do I feel?
- Where do these feelings come from?
- Why do I think I experience them?
- How are they useful to me?

- What do I see as the consequences of their continuation?
- What are other times I have felt similarly?
- What do I need to re-experience and amplify?

What is appreciative action?

We suggest that learning through appreciative reflection involves the qualities of awareness, astuteness and alignment.

1. *Awareness:* This concerns reflecting not only on what is but also what might be. It involves utilizing what it is we currently know as a creative springboard, to unleash our imagination in order to envision doing things differently. Having said this, healthcare professionals still have to exercise their judgement with regard to what is best and for whom. A key question becomes, 'How can busy clinicians or managers improve their levels of awareness?' A good way to begin is to reflect upon our openness to experience and the courage and opportunity we have to 'play' with new and different ways of working. In other words the freedom we have (or otherwise) to explore new ways of practising. So how can the healthcare professional take or risk the time for such reflection?

2. *Astuteness:* This is about our ability to interpret, organise and pragmatically use the fruits arising from awareness. Another way to express this latter attribute is implementation. Appreciative reflection is a strengths-based approach to improving healthcare practice and policy. So it follows that we need to be very astute in order to achieve this. Our political acuity and skilfulness at influencing others, plays a big part in implementing something that we feel will lead to improvements in aspects of healthcare. Astuteness is closely associated with empowerment and our awareness of organizational power and politics. The choice of implementation strategies in healthcare is not a value-free choice of course.

3. *Alignment:* This focuses on the match (or congruence) between what we say and what we actually do. It also concerns the way individual values match with organizational ones. Appreciative action of this kind is a way of understanding our personal relationship with our job. When there is a good alignment, there is synergy between personal and organizational needs. There is a balance between individual and organizational direction. This presupposes, of course, that the individual healthcare worker actually knows the direction in which the organization of moving.

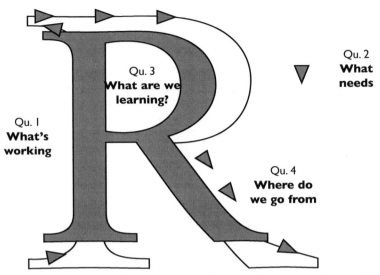

Figure 1.2. An appreciative reflective learning framework. (see also Ghaye 2009 for more details).

A framework for appreciative reflection

The positive (improvement) questions we are suggesting that could usefully form the basis of experiencing appreciative reflection are shown in *Figure 1.2*. The four core questions are both generative and appreciative.

An elaboration of each question is;

1. What's currently working well and why?
2. What needs changing and how?
3. What are you/we learning and so what do we need to do next?
4. Where do you/we go from here and what are the implications for improving your/our future clinical and managerial action and organizational culture/s?

We suggest that question 1 is a good place to start any improvement process. Reflecting on it means actively and consciously starting the improvement process by looking at what is positive and supportive of human flourishing and well-being in current thinking and practice. It is an appreciation of our own and others' gifts and talents. It is a focus on positivity. Question 2 is essentially about using our awareness and astuteness in trying to envision better ways of working. For some this may include looking at 'problems' (or challenges) creatively and with a critical spirit in order to seek out alternative and innovative approaches for future practice. It involves being open to the unexpected connection. Question 3 is about improving working practices and workplaces through the authentic participant ownership of issues. It requires the suspension of status games that undermine the creativity of the work group or healthcare team, and a focus on ways to build more practical wisdom. It also requires the skilful use of language and the way participants use their different kinds of authority in the company of others. The practical wisdom we have in mind is not simply the outcome of reproductive thinking. In other words, simply refining what is already known. It seeks to generate new insights and improved actions. In this sense we might call it productive thinking. Question 4 involves both astuteness and alignment. It is the principled and pragmatic ways in which we might implement what it is we feel stands a good chance of improving some aspect of practice or policy.

Here are some further examples of the kinds of positive questions, with a strong appreciative (and reflective) tone, that we have in mind. How do you react to them?

1. What is giving you most joy and satisfaction in your work right now?
2. What were you doing recently, in managing your time, that enabled you to use your strengths?
3. What actions were you taking when you were successful at prioritizing those things that you are really good at doing?
4. What was happening when you found yourself thinking, that really worked well?
5. What did someone say or do to make you feel that your professional experience was greatly appreciated?
6. What strengths do you feel you have to 'fight fires' at work? (Fire fighting is about constantly fixing problems and dealing with what's urgent rather than what might be important.)
7. What did you do that prompted a colleague to say 'Thank you, it's nice to be respected'?
8. What were you doing that prompted a colleague to say 'It's great working here, it's nice to be valued'?
9. What did you say to a colleague that enabled them to say 'Thanks for understanding my situation'? (Ghaye et al 2008)

The benefits that can arise from appreciative reflection come about through our conversations with others. The words we choose to use. The questions we decide to ask and the way we hear and then decide to respond. This means it is us who play an integral part in what we learn through reflection. It is us who determines the extent of the shift away from deficit-based conversations and towards more strengths-based ones; conversations that bring joy, wellness and positive engagement into all our healthcare work.

References

Boud, D. Cressey, P. & Docherty, P. (2006) Productive reflection at work: learning for changing organizations. Taylor and Francis.

Cooperrider, D. (2001) Working Paper: Appreciative Inquiry: Releasing the Power of the Positive Question, Case Western Reserve University Cleveland, OH United States, Available online at: http://appreciativeinquiry.case.edu/uploads/working_paper_AI_and_power_positive_question.pdf.

Cooperrider, D. L., & Srivastva, S. (1987) Appreciative inquiry in organizational life, In, Pasmore, W. A. & Woodman, R. W. (Eds.), Research in Organizational Change and Development (Vol. 1). JAI Press, Greenwich, CT.

Dewey, J. (1933) *How We Think: A Restatement of the Relation of Reflective Thinking to the Educative Process*. Heath & Company, Lexington, M.A.

Ghaye, T (2009) *In what ways can reflective practices enhance human flourishing?* Reflective Practice, 11 (1) 1-7.

Ghaye, T. (2005) Developing the Reflective Healthcare Team. Blackwell, Oxford.

Ghaye, T. & Lillyman, S. (2006) Learning Journals and Critical Incidents: Reflective Practice for Health Care Professionals, Mark Allen Publications. 2nd Edition.

Ghaye, T., Melander-Wikman, A., Kisare, M., Chambers, P., Bergmark, U., Kostenius, C. and Lillyman, S. (2008) Participatory and appreciative action and reflection (PAAR) – democratizing reflective practices. Reflective Practice, 9 (4) 361–397.

Kaufka, B. (2009) The shadows within: Internalized racism and reflective writing, Reflective Practice, 10 (2) 137-148.

Ling, A et al (2008) *An evaluation of the Health Foundation's Engaging with Quality Initiative: Third annual report,* The Health Foundation, London.

Loughran, J. (2006) A response to 'Reflecting on the self'. Reflective Practice, 7 (1) 43-53.

Marchi, S & Ghaye, T (2010) *Appreciative Reflection: How to feel positive and do good work*. New Vista Publications, Gloucester. Forthcoming.

Øvretveit, J. (2009) Leading improvement effectively. The Health Foundation.

Raelin, J.A. (2008) Work-Based Learning: Bridging knowledge and action in the workplace (new and revised edition) Jossey-Bass, San Francisco.

Schön, D (1983) The Reflective Practitioner: how professionals think in action. Basic Books, New York.

Schön, D.A. (ed.) (1991) The Reflective Turn. Teachers College Press, New York.

Stavros J & Torres C, (2006) Dynamic Relationships: Unleashing the power of appreciative inquiry in daily living, Taos Institute Publication, Chagrin Falls, Ohio.

CHAPTER 2

Kyoko — learning from a patient

In this chapter we want to establish the first and second 'principles' of reflective practice. (Other principles are introduced as they arise naturally in the chapters throughout the book.)

> Principle 1: Reflective practice is about you and your work

Reflection begins with thinking again about what we do with and for others. We reflect on what we think and feel about our healthcare work. It starts and ends with practice. Through reflection we can come to know more about what we do, why we do it 'that' way and what might serve to limit our ability to care in a certain fashion. By reflecting on what we do we also provide ourselves with opportunities for improving aspects of our work. Healthcare practice operates within a 'context'. All sorts of things can make this context either a happy and rewarding one in which to work, or a depressing and difficult one. So when we reflect-on-practice we reflect on what we did, or think we did, as well as on what we might, should or could have done. The 'context' in which we practice is a big influence on all of this.

One of the things we can do in learning through the 'caring moment' which follows (see Ghaye and Lillyman 2000, for an explanation of this idea), is to begin to establish a vocabulary which healthcare professionals might usefully employ when trying to reflect-on-practice, either individually or collectively. What follows is also a clear illustration of Principle 1. We reflect on practice. We create some kind of 'text' or record of it. This is the raw material, if you like, which we use in many different ways. It enables us to think again, to learn from our experiences and (hopefully) it energizes our commitment to strive continuously to improve what we do. We are greatly indebted to Brenda Landgrebe for allowing us to share her story of Kyoko with you.

Kyoko — learning from a patient

Kyoko was beautiful. She stood quite still by the window of the bedroom as I entered. She was wearing a simple shift dress which fell to her knees. Her arms were bare, slightly bronzed and very slim. Her wrists and hands were tiny; her fingers laced together at waist height. Her legs were slim but shapely and her feet, like her hands, were very small and were clad in thonged sandals anchored at a point between each first and second toe.

I looked at her face. Slightly arched, narrow black eyebrows accentuated deep, black-lashed, almond-shaped eyes. High, rounded cheekbones supported faint shadows which further enhanced their prominence. A small flat nose, testifying to her antecedents, sat above full pale lips. Her hair was blue-black and glossy, parted at the centre of her head and tucked behind her ears to fall straight down her back. When she stepped towards me I could see that it reached almost to the hem of her dress.

She smiled; a small, hesitant, gentle smile which hardly disturbed her serene countenance but which signalled nevertheless untold emotions — timidity, warmth, fear and confusion.

Kyoko was beautiful and she was dying.

I had been asked to visit Kyoko in my capacity as continuing care nurse. As is customary, the referring general practitioner had given me the information I needed to make a first visit.

Kyoko was 36 years old and had had a recurrence of breast cancer which had been treated initially in the Philippines. She had had a mastectomy and chemotherapy. Eighteen months later, cancer was diagnosed in the remaining breast and it was decided that she would come to England for further treatment and to be with her husband who was studying here. Although from the Philippines, Kyoko was of Japanese origin. Her husband was also Japanese. Kyoko was going to live in the house of her husband's brother and his French wife, whilst receiving treatment.

During our first conversation I discovered that Kyoko had been to the local general hospital and, following tests, had been told that the cancer was well advanced and that further curative treatment was not feasible although she would remain under the supervision of the doctors at the hospital.

She spoke excellent English and there was no doubt that she had understood the significance of the doctor's remarks. Kyoko did not cry, did not express any anger but merely told me the facts.

We discussed her present physical condition, spending a short time on those symptoms which appeared minor (in Kyoko's perception), such as nausea, and a longer time on those that she considered important, such as pain.

After I had ensured that Kyoko understood how and when to take her drugs and had given her a contact number, we came to a joint decision that I would visit once a week for the time being but that Kyoko would telephone if she needed to see me sooner. I told Kyoko that I would speak to her sister-in-law before I left the house.

Nicole met me at the foot of the stairs and asked when Kyoko was going to be taken into hospital. We went into the sitting room and I explained that Kyoko did not need to be in hospital right then but that she could go into hospital when this was needed.

Nicole felt that she had been misled by her Japanese in-laws concerning the seriousness of Kyoko's condition. She felt, she said, angry that she was expected to accept the responsibility. While she had been prepared for differences to emerge between her husband's culture and her own when they married, she could not and would not accept that she should not be consulted about such a major event as a stranger dying in her home.

I let her talk. It transpired that she had had some problems in her marriage, first with the in-laws advising their son — 'telling him what we should do' was how she put it — but since the birth of their daughter things had not been so bad. She thought the family had accepted that she had a mind of her own. 'But now this,' she sighed. Leaving my contact number and promising that I would do all I could to help, I left the house, feeling sorry for both of the women in it.

Throughout the couple of months that I knew Kyoko she did not complain about anything. If her pain worsened, she waited until I made a regular visit to her to tell me, or Nicole asked me to visit.

At one point, the hospital consultant decided that another course of chemotherapy might delay the progress of the disease, so this was tried. Kyoko reacted violently to the treatment, vomiting almost continuously and was unable to eat or drink. She was already losing weight with terrifying speed, was very tired and had gross muscle weakness and, despite changes in her drug regime, when her anti-emetic drugs were either increased or alternatives tried, the vomiting continued. The chemotherapy was discontinued.

During this time, Nicole telephoned frequently and I visited often, sometimes alone, at other times with the general practitioner. At each visit Nicole became more voluble, demanding that we 'do something'. Usually she calmed down enough to agree to Kyoko staying at the house for the time being, but it was obvious to the doctor and myself that if the situation became any worse, Kyoko would have to be admitted to hospital or a hospice unit.

She, however, despite the vomiting and the weakness, remained calm. She continued to care for herself, never wanting to give Nicole any trouble, and did not stay in bed for any length of time. In fact I never saw her in bed but always sitting in a chair and always dressed. Only once did she express her dismay at what was happening to her. I arrived to find her sitting in front of the mirror brushing her beautiful hair. Her expression was very sad and when I asked her what was wrong, she held up the brush for me to see. Long black strands were matted in the bristles.

'My hair is coming out,' she said. 'My husband does not want to see me like this.'

Eventually , Kyoko's condition dictated that she should be admitted to hospital. I went to see her, just once as it turned out, before she died. Ever respectful she apologized for not being able to get out of bed and admitted that she was 'very weary'.

She talked then of her husband and their families, of Nicole, of the doctors who had tried to help her and of me. She had not been able to be a 'good' wife for her husband, she said, and she had disappointed both sets of parents because she had not given them a grandchild. Nicole had given her a home and she had made a lot of extra work for her. She was sorry for the trouble she had given the doctors and myself. Everyone had been so kind, given so much, but her body had not been strong enough to get better.

Before I left her she held my hand briefly and thanked me again. She had never voluntarily touched me during our short time of knowing each other and this simple gesture was her gift to me. I never saw her again. Kyoko died less than two days later.

No amount of theoretical knowledge can prepare any practitioner to cope with the variety of situations and events with which he or she will be presented.

Every effort is made to ensure that adequate preparation is given to the practitioner before he or she practises in specific areas. Nurses involved with the care of dying individuals may choose from several courses validated by professional or academic bodies, or experiential workshops where they can learn about the physical, psychological, social and spiritual problems which may be experienced by the dying person, and also examine their own feelings and reactions to death. Such courses are also designed to assist practitioners to improve their knowledge and skills in order to help those individuals in a constructive manner.

Not only had I attended a course aptly named 'Care of the dying patient and the family' in which these issues were addressed, but I had also been to a series of study days, arranged by an organization founded by Margaret Torrie (herself a doctor's widow), where issues surrounding all aspects were examined.

Armed, then, with knowledge and skills which I deemed more than adequate to cope with any situation concerning dying people, I was confident that I could help Kyoko during her last few weeks of life.

However, to have knowledge in theory alone is not only limiting to both practitioners and patient, but it can be damaging to both.

Most nurses can quote the 'psychological stages' that a dying patient goes through, as described by Elizabeth Kubler-Ross (1970), — denial, anger, depression, acceptance — but the pitfall here might be that the nurse remembers the book and forgets to study the individual. In an attempt to 'stage' the patient, the individual needs of the dying person may well be overlooked.

My own initial reactions to Kyoko's situation reflected more accurately Kubler-Ross' stages than did Kyoko's. I could not believe (denial) that so many bad things could happen to one person. An apparently loveless marriage, a strange country, an irate kinswoman, a recurrence of cancer, then sterility following chemotherapy, and the prospect of death. My own inner feelings (anger) made me want to stop some, if not all, of these things from happening to her. I perceived her to be vulnerable and this made me feel extremely sad (depression?).

All of these feelings, however, were fleeting. Kyoko's own calm acceptance of her situation was infectious. From our first meeting to the last her serenity influenced not only my relationship with her, but ultimately relationships with patients and others to this day. I learned from Kyoko what theorists, writers and lecturers could never teach me. That each individual with whom we have contact as practitioners can add a new dimension to our lives, even while we believe that we are teaching them.

Kyoko, whilst making use of my knowledge and experience especially concerning the use of drugs to control her distressing symptoms, taught me that no matter what my feelings were about a situation, I should in no way impose those feelings on another and, indeed, in Kyoto's case her own attitude towards her circumstance could not be influenced.

Socrates is quoted as saying,

> ... we shall be better, braver and more active men if we believe it right to look for what we don't know than if we believe there is no point in looking because what we don't know we can never discover.

After Kyoko's death, I made a promise to myself that I would, in future, not only resist prejudging any situation but that I would endeavour to learn something new from each patient I met.

(Printed here with the kind permission of Brenda Landgrebe and Richard Winter for and on behalf of the editors of the *Educational Action Research Journal* in which it was originally published.)

Reflecting-on-practice

If we reflect on this humanly significant encounter between a nurse and her patient, we find there is much for us to learn about how we might begin to reflect on practice. We need to have something on which to reflect. We cannot reflect on every aspect of what we do. We have to be selective and choose to work on the 'significant' bits of it. This is easier said than done. What is significant now may not be next week. Similarly, what might be regarded as a part of our ordinary, taken-for-granted, everyday routine work may in fact become highly significant at a later date. The bottom line is that we need to have a good reason to think again about some aspect of our work. We should be clear about what this reason is. We should avoid reflecting only on the extraordinary. The ordinary deserves attention also.

In this 'caring moment' with Kyoko, there are *people* and *actions*. Both are located within a *context* — a home, a hospital — at a given time and also within a social and cultural context. There is a *thinking* (or cognitive) element to it as reflected, for example, in the decisions being made about Kyoko's care. There is an *emotional* (or affective) dimension to the 'moment' as expressed, for example, in Kyoko's wishes and hopes and in Nicole's misgivings and worries. Taken together, what we have here are some of the basic elements of being able to learn through reflective practice.

We can reflect again on this and learn even more. In thinking again we are making the point that reflective practice is a *continuous learning process*, not something we simply pick up, drop, and then pick up again three months later. When we reflect on practice we should seek to dig down a bit and try to get below the surface of the practice incident. Reflective practice is indeed about *looking into something*, literally. There are a number of processes and methods to help us to do just this. Two common ones are through the process of critical incident analysis and journal writing (Ghaye and Lillyman, 1999)

In the story of Kyoko, what is revealed to us is the way reflection helps us to *account for ourselves*. Brenda, the nurse involved, is not only describing what she did but she is also giving reasons for her actions. For example, in listening to and discussing Kyoko's condition with Nicole, Brenda is able to explain and justify to herself (and to others) what she is doing and feeling and why. Brenda is also reflecting on and using her *experience* in order to come to an understanding of the degree to which she is able to claim that she is caring in a safe and competent manner. She has her own practice knowledge and experience to draw upon, as well as the knowledge from all the courses she has attended. Brenda is also showing a certain *disposition* to enquire into her practice, hence this story and her commitment and skill in placing it in the public domain. Another part of this disposition is reflected in the way Brenda, latterly, tries to make sense of her own 'reactions to Kyoko's situation'. Brenda also engages in and manages to sustain a number of conversations. Her principle conversations are with Kyoko and Nicole. They are *reflective conversations* (see *Chapter 5*) in that they discuss values. For example, the things Kyoko values, and the caring values Brenda is trying to live out in her practice. It is through reflective conversations that we can tease apart the 'caring moments' we live through, and in so doing, give ourselves the opportunity to understand even better our struggles to realize holistic caring.

In this way, reflection-on-practice is about the process of *making sense* of practice. We make sense of things in different ways (this is the focus of another book in this series entitled, *Caring Moments: The discourse of reflective practice*). This is not a simple process. In the Kyoko story, Brenda makes a number of decisions (some of them joint ones) about, for example, the number of times each week she would visit Kyoko and Nicole. Through being with and listening to both of them, Brenda decodes what is it they are saying, or she thinks they are saying. In *decoding*, she is trying to make sense of the whole situation in which Kyoko's continuing care is central. She tries to make sense of what they are saying and then she *constructs* some kind of personal set of meanings and understandings about the developing situation. This forms the basis for what she does in the future; for how she plans for and sustains Kyoko's care.

There are some big messages here. Brenda's story makes a hugely significant point about reflection-on-practice. From one caring moment, if we can think about it in particular ways, we can learn a great deal. We do not have to reflect on everything, on lots of practice incidents. The story of Kyoko helps us to appreciate that less is often more. We need to learn as much as we can from our chosen aspect of practice. Often we do not have the time, motivation or skills to reflect on many different things all at once. Brenda's story is also an example of a *reflective turn* (Schön 1991). This means that through her writing, Brenda is returning to look closely at this particular 'moment' (Johns 1997). Re-encountering in this way is likely to challenge some of Brenda's assumptions, feelings and understandings. This is evident, for example, in the denial and anger that she feels about Kyoko's situation and in her trying to manage sensitively the feelings and requests of Kyoko's sister-in-law.

We can link Kyoko's story to three other fundamental ideas about reflective practice. The first is that we need a reason to reflect on practice. Reflection normally serves a particular purpose. It also serves certain interests. We might conclude that Brenda is reflecting on her practice because this is very much part of her commitment to care. It is a professional value that she lives out as a continuing care nurse. There are many other interests being served here as well, but are some interests also being denied? Secondly, Brenda may also feel that reflecting-on-practice in this way helps her to improve what she does because, through reflective writing, she has deepened her understanding of what she does and of what she can, might or even should do in future circumstances of this kind. This deeper and richer understanding of her practice may enable her to feel more *empowered to act* in a particular direction in the future (see another book in this series entitled, *Empowerment Through Reflection: The narratives of healthcare professionals*). It may also be reassuring. Brenda may feel that her actions were both competent and ethical in the circumstances and that she really would not change anything substantially if she were to be confronted with this particular configuration of care again. In other words, reflection-on-practice enables Brenda to establish, justify and reaffirm some generic principles and practices of care. Finally, Brenda may feel that through her reflective writing she is more *enlightened*, as she constantly weighs up the match between what and how she cares for others and how far she is allowed or enabled to care given the contexts in which she works. Put another way, reflection-on-practice can act as a bridge between Brenda's own *'theories'* of care, how she puts these theories to use in her practice, and how *practice modifies and transforms her theories* over time.

When we say, as Principle 1, that reflective practice is about you and your work, we therefore mean that it involves at least:

People	For example, patients, clients, managers, families, healthcare professionals
Thinking and emotions	That is, cognitions and feelings.
Action	For example, action which is intentional, committed and informed by the best evidence available to us.
Context	This is physically where the action takes place and occurs over time. Context also has social and political aspects to it.
Accountability	Being able to account for our clinical, managerial and professional actions. This involves description, explanation and justification.
Experience	We reflect on our experience (and that of others). This is what we have done, thought about and envisioned. It is the 'raw material' for reflective practice.
Disposition	Reflection is not a toolbox, but rather a set of principles and practices which help us to see more clearly, deeply and richly.

Conversation	We learn, for example, through observing, listening and conversing. The reflective conversation is at the heart of a commitment to try to improve practice.
Sense-making	This is where we use our powers of analysis, synthesis and evaluation, in some structured and supported manner, to enhance our understanding of care.
Building	Better understandings can help us to make wiser and more principled clinical decisions. Reflection-on-practice is about building (or constructing) better understandings.
Reflective turns	Reflection needs to be understood as a continuous learning process. It involves re-seeing, re-experiencing, re-viewing and re-searching what it is we do in order to develop a more holistic view of care.
Empowerment	This, at least, means coming to know, being able to express and critically analyse our own healthcare realities, and having a sense of control over them.
Theories	Reflection helps us to develop our own theories-of-action and to assess the usefulness of other people's theories, all of which help to guide our practice and account for what we do.

In commenting on 'Kyoko — learning from a patient', Winter (in Landgrebe and Winter, 1994) makes the following observations:

1. The 'story' format can make practice accessible to the reader.
2. Brenda's is an example of a reflective narrative. As such, it is a particular form of representation which allows certain understandings to emerge and be known.
3. Through writing we can come to terms with experience and new insights can be given the chance to emerge.
4. Learning through reflection and reflective writing does have professional and clinical consequences. For Brenda, these were to do with cultural differences in attitudes to illness and health, with an increased concern for trying to understand why her patients (some of

whom were dying) acted in the way they did and with discovering what, for her, was a new way of communicating to others something about her practice.

We can therefore conclude this chapter by expressing a second principle, which is:

Principle 2: Reflective practice is about learning from experience

This illuminates reflection as being a conscious and intentional activity. Brenda's final observation reinforces the point. She says:

After Kyoko's death, I made a promise to myself that I would, in future, not only resist prejudging any situation, but that I would endeavour to learn something new from each patient I met.

References

Ghaye T, Lillyman S (1999) *Learning Journals and Critical Incidents:Reflective Practice for Health Care Professionals*. Mark Allen Publishing Group, Salisbury

Ghaye T, Lillyman S (2000) *Caring Moments: The discourse of reflective practice*. Mark Alien Publishing Group, Salisbury

Johns, C (1997) Reflective Practice and Clinical Supervision — Part 1:The Reflective Turn. *European Nurse* **2** (2): 87-97

Kubler-Ross E (1970) *On Death and Dying*. Tavistock, London

Landgrebe B, Winter R (1994) *Reflective Writing on Practice:Professional support for the dying*. Educ Action Res Jl (I): 83-94

Schon D, ed. (1991) The Reflective Turn: Case studies in and on educational practice. Teachers College Press, New York

CHAPTER 3

Reflection on experience: Whose knowledge is worth knowing?

In the previous chapter we were arguing that through reflection we are able to turn experience into learning (Boud et al 1998).The story of Kyoko also illustrates the point that reflection and experience are mutually enhancing (Heron 1998). They need each other. In this chapter we intend to explore three further principles of reflective practice. The first is:

> **Principle 3: Reflective practice is about valuing what we do and why we do it**

It is likely that, in the context of the Department of Health (2008) *A High Quality Workforce; NHS next stage review*, it will become increasingly necessary to ask questions about 'What knowledge' and 'Whose knowledge is worth knowing'. These are complex questions to answer and this is by implication, therefore, a complex chapter. In trying to answer the 'knowledge questions', we will explore three areas. Firstly, the idea of 'knowledge about and for clinical action'. Secondly, we will take a look at that kind of knowledge which is 'theoretical' and thirdly, we will try to join these two ideas together and discuss the ways in which practice and theory link up and need each other. In discussing these tricky knowledge (or epistemological) questions we should not lose sight of our third 'principle', namely that being committed to reflective practice means having a commitment to value that kind of knowledge which we shall call 'personal-practical knowledge'. This knowledge is derived from the local, complex, diverse, dynamic and unpredictable realities of both individuals and groups of healthcare professionals working in particular clinical environments.

It's party time!

Imagine that you are at a friend's birthday party. You know some of the guests, but not everyone. As the room fills, you edge over to the mantelpiece where a piece of 'pop art' catches your eye. It attracts the attention of another guest at nearly the same time.

'An interesting type of candle holder,' you say cheerfully, although this is actually a wild guess.

'A candle holder?' he replies with gentle surprise. 'It's a bud vase… or at least I think it is!'

'Oh, you think so? I wonder. It's rather nice, whatever it is.'

You both sip your drinks rather nervously, wondering what on earth you might say next. A conversation on sculptures and sculpting hardly seems likely to be one that you could sustain. But, just before the gap in your conversation becomes a gaping chasm of silence, he gets in first with, 'And what do you do then?'

'Oh,' you say, very grateful for this lifesaving conversation filler. 'I work in healthcare.'

As soon as you say it you feel that he expects much more than that. He doesn't have to ask the next question, but he does.

'Oh, really? That's interesting. So what do you do then?'

We wonder exactly how you might develop this conversation. Fundamentally, at this imaginary party, you have been asked a 'knowledge question'. Knowledge questions, of various kinds, are asked and answered in our caring work every day. They reveal something about the purposes, practices and outcomes of healthcare work. They illuminate what we think, feel and value. Knowledge questions also set up discussions about the battles, struggles and controversies in healthcare concerning:

- What it means to know about nursing, or health visiting, or speech and language therapy, and so on.
- Who has the power, authority and skills to generate useful knowledge.
- How this knowledge should or might be used.
- Whose and what interests are being served when we monitor and evaluate the impact of this knowledge on patients.

In this chapter we argue that individuals and groups of healthcare practitioners themselves — the clinicians, those practising care — are uniquely placed to know about healthcare work, and that they can and should be seen as both generators and users of knowledge. They do not have to generate knowledge alone. Where appropriate they should seek the help of others in allied professions and from collaborating or partnership organizations, for example in higher education. We will also suggest that the knowledge they generate is developed through reflective practice and is worthwhile knowledge.

This is not to say that knowledge is 'merely' local and deeply embedded in an immediate healthcare context. We will argue that this knowledge, which we are calling 'personal-practical', can also be relevant and useful to the wider healthcare community. This is congruent with our view that reflective practice is not just a private and solitary occupation. We believe that it must also be seen as a public and shared activity. In this sense, then, personal-practical knowledge is derived from participating in, and reflecting on, action. Such knowledge is experiential because it values the world of experience. It is also public — shared, and consequently critiqued, by peers. It is therefore about making sense of, and giving meaning to, practice.

Knowledge for safe and accountable clinical practice

We can begin with the idea that clinical practice is guided by three kinds of knowledge. These kinds of knowledge enable us to make claims firstly to 'know that' something is the case, secondly to 'know how' to do something and thirdly to 'know why' we practise in the way we do. 'Know that' knowledge is often called factual or propositional knowledge. 'Know how' knowledge is to do with the skills and competencies which we need and use in our work. 'Know why' knowledge is a values-based knowledge. The values we hold and subscribe to give us the reasons why we do what we do and in the particular ways we do it (see *Chapter 7*). Yaxley (1991) raises two pertinent questions about the knowledge which professionals claim to hold. These are:

1. How do we come to know what we claim to know about competent practice?
2. How do we justify making these claims?

He goes on to suggest that (p.1)

> *:... the answer to the first question will be a claim about how we learn or personally construct knowledge... whilst the second question must be answered in terms of how we justify the claim to have developed new knowledge.*

Another way of responding to these questions is to reaffirm that it is through systematic and rigorous reflection-on-practice that we come to know, and to justify, what we know.

There has been a great deal of material written about the nature of healthcare, and nursing knowledge in particular (Carper 1978, Jenks 1993, Palmer, Burns and Bulman 1994, Chinn and Kramer 1995, White 1995, Benner et al 1996, Johns and Freshwater 2005).

Where knowledge comes from and how useful it is seen to be, is often a source of tension and confusion. Part of this is because there are so many views on the issue and so many ways of labelling knowledge. Griffiths (1998) describes this clearly. For example, in addition to the three types of knowledge described above, we can think of Lyotard's (1984):

...distinction between knowledge which can be commodified and a range of other kinds of knowledge. Knowledge which can commodified is either 'information', which can be expressed in bytes of information, or 'competence', which can be measured against the yardstick of efficiency.
Other kinds of knowledge are those which are organized around language games not only of truth and of efficiency but also of ethical wisdom (justice and/or happiness) and beauty (auditory and visual sensibility).

These ideas are very important in any thinking or discussion about the knowledge base which guides any professional's work, which gives a profession its identity, confidence and sense of maturity. It also informs the continuing debate about nursing, health visiting, midwifery and a range of professions allied to medicine being 'artful', 'scientific' and/or even 'pseudo-scientific' in nature (Newell 1994).

There are also other kinds of knowledge relevant to healthcare professionals, which say something important about the kind of knowledge generated through reflection. Foucault (1980) used the term, 'subjugated knowledges'. This opens up the whole debate in healthcare about some kinds of knowledge being more privileged and of higher status than others. In Foucault's terms, subjugated knowledge is particular and 'regional', marginal and subordinate to, for example, the knowledge of medicine and other knowledge further up the hierarchy of respectability and science. Knowledge of the daily behaviours of healthcare professionals (narratives) and knowledge generated through reflective conversations (see *Chapter 6*) would both be examples of 'subjugated knowledge'.

Arguably, we should know something about four further kinds of knowledge. They are all pertinent to healthcare and to reflective practice. Firstly, Rose's (1994) idea of 'responsible knowledge' is knowledge influenced by love and care. Secondly, Griffiths' (1998) notion of 'better knowledge' (p.129):

> *This is better knowledge in two senses of 'better': knowledge which can be relied on and knowledge which can be used wisely, to a good purpose.*

Thirdly, there is a phrase, increasingly heard in healthcare, namely 'outsider knowledge'. This refers to knowledge 'out there', detached from us, not owned by us but which impacts on us 'in here'. The most obvious illustrations are Government reports, policies and visions which emanate from the 'centre', and research papers produced by those in the 'academy'. In order to understand and use this outsider knowledge, for example to improve our clinical work, we must find ways to gain access to and understand it. The task is made all the more difficult if the knowledge is written in a language which we have little experience of decoding — especially, for example, statistical language. Finally, there is the helpful view of knowledge offered by Polanyi (1958) and labelled 'personal knowledge'. This is often unconscious and 'hidden'. We have it but we might not know we do! It is often hard to put words to it. Sometimes we call personal knowledge 'tacit'. It is tacit knowledge because we often have to infer it from clinical actions and statements. According to Sternberg and Horvath (1999), knowledge of this kind is the key to intelligent behaviour in practical settings. It is a practical kind of knowledge which we need in order to work in a safe, ethical and accountable way. This tacit or personal knowledge, then, is:

- intimately related to what we do (action)
- relevant to the attainment of standards and goals which we set ourselves and value
- something which we develop and construct for ourselves
- not the only kind of knowledge which we need!

'A world behind masks': An example of personal-practical knowledge

There are many courses which value learning from experience, where the participating healthcare professionals are invited to research their professional self and healthcare practice. This can be done in many ways, such as learning through journal writing (Ghaye and Lillyman 2006). In a paper entitled *The Power of Narrative: 'transcending disciplines'*, Gartner et al (1996) describe how they engage their nursing students, on a postgraduate Certificate in Critical Care Nursing course, in journalising. Students on the course write about their experiences in practice, in their journals, for one hour per week throughout the semester. Interestingly (p.8):

...in self-selected groups of three or four, each member in turn, reads a practice scenario from their journal entry and leads the group in a critical analysis of it. Throughout discussions 'critical peers' play a vital role in providing the necessary feedback that enables group members to work towards becoming critical, reflective practitioners.

What follows below is an extract from a student's journal. It not only captures the uniqueness of peri-operative nursing, but is also an example of what we mean when we use the term 'personal-practical' knowledge. We thank Anne, Gloria and Susan for allowing us to share this with you.

A world behind masks

The surgeon stared at me with eyes that could have pierced glaciers, no warmth and no smile in them... maybe he was concentrating. Standing there scrubbed, my eyes shifted quickly to seek out another pair... the next set were just as bad, they were serious and cold... I felt their tension. I stood motionless, my eyes darted around. I was shopping for silent conversation from eyes that were affirming, eyes that could tell me that 'it's OK'. Where are those bloody eyes? Then I looked down at the patient. She was pale and tiny. Her eyes weren't sparkling... they were moist, cloudy and grey.... full of fear..... The surgery begins. I look at the surgeon... my trolley, I need confirmation. I watch the surgeon's eyes watching me, I stare back, he raises his eyebrows, not in a puzzled manner but in a comforting way...Ah... I'm relieved... I must be performing OK... then I remembered the patient's eyes.

Earlier on we began to describe some of the qualities of 'personal-practical knowledge' derived from reflective practice. We said that tied up with reflection was a public process of the discussion of caring moments (or of practice incidents) in supportive and yet constructively critical peer groups. This is another part of a sense-making phase where we can attribute added meaning to that aspect of practice being reflected upon. The student shared her experience, cited above, in such company. This led to a further journal entry some time later.

In thinking about the meaning of my story.... The eyes of theatre are powerful. They communicate emotion and hide no truths. I thought about how many times eyes, without verbal communication, have been instructive to me. For example, eyes have told me that I've assembled the Finichietto retractor back to front... . Eyes have said that your trolley and Mayo stand are the best set up in town... .

Eyes have also told me that my eight questions about the surgical procedure are just about enough!... I thought about all the cues that I get from my patient's eyes. They tell me about their fears, their strengths, their apprehensions, their vulnerability... How does my gaze communicate messages to my patient? Are my gazes caring? Do I say with my eyes, 'It will be OK'... 'You're in safe hands'... 'I care about what happens to you'? Do they convey a sense of security, empathy, comfort, hope...? Peri-operative nurses should never underestimate the power of their gaze, especially in a world behind masks.

We have also suggested that this 'personal-practical' knowledge can also be of relevance and use to the wider healthcare community. For example, from this practice incident Gartner, Latham and Merrit (1996) suggest that the generation of such knowledge can:

- Help nurses to understand more richly what it means to be responsive or connected as they try to articulate an ethic of care.
- Provide a framework for understanding people because they expose how experiences are endowed with meaning.
- Celebrate the importance of narrative forms of representation and, in doing so, value the healthcare professional as narrator (teller), observer, holder of knowledge, and expert.

Is there a sixth way?

So far in this chapter we have been exploring the third principle of reflective practice and the way in which it values personal-practical knowledge. Through valuing such knowledge, we may come to have a more holistic and deeper awareness of the basis of our clinical work, and of how past experiences affect present behaviour and future hopes. The knowledge we are describing here derives from the links between our personal life-history and our professional/clinical careers. In this way, 'experience', 'self' and 'others' become the key elements in personal-practical knowledge. Burns and Grove (1993) put the case that the nursing profession, for example, has historically acquired knowledge through five principal modes. These are: tradition, authority, borrowing, trial and error and role modelling.

Tradition

A tradition is something that has been in existence for a long time.It is a way of doing things from the past which affects current practice. Department, ward and unit 'cultures' are often built around certain traditions or accepted ways of doing things. Sometimes traditional behaviours are hard to change, particularly if they are supported by people in positions of power and authority. When improvements to clinical areas need to be made, traditional beliefs and actions have to be questioned. This can be uncomfortable for those involved. It can also be liberating if all are prepared to consider alternative ways of working. Reflection-on-practice fuels this kind of discussion amongst clinicians.

Authority

We often hear people use the expression: 'She's an authority on the matter'. Authority has something to do with knowledge, expertise and power. Healthcare knowledge comes from various authorities, for example, Benner (1984) is often regarded as an authority. She argues that the amount of personal experience we have affects the amount and quality of the knowledge base we can draw upon. In her seminal work, she describes five different levels of experience in the development of clinical knowledge and expertise. These are from novice to advanced beginner, to competent, proficient and finally expert levels. Some interesting parallels can be drawn between the work of Benner (1984) and that reported by Burrows (1994). Both provide developmental schemas that relate to the learner's cognitive maturity and increasing expertise. Burrows reports on research which indicates that nursing students work through four different developmental phases. In each phase they hold a particular view of knowledge, as follows:

The *dualist* phase: where knowledge is seen as right or wrong and where tutors try to provide all the 'correct' answers to problems.

The *multiplicity* phase: where learners appreciate that people hold different opinions about the same thing.

The *relativist* phase: where learners recognise that different opinions may have different degrees of worth.

The *commitment* phase: where learners construct their own knowledge bases in relation to their own practices.

In the works of Benner (1984), Burrows (1994) and also Carper (1978), another figure widely regarded as an authority, there is an acknowledgement of the value of personal-practical knowledge. Apart from the value of reading her original work, Carper's four 'patterns of knowing' within nursing are summarized elsewhere (Basford and Slavin 1995, Christensen and Kenney 1995, Ghaye and Lillyman 2006). Carper characterizes knowledge as that which helps us to know ourselves better and also that which helps us to interpret and make sense of the social contexts in which we practise. She makes links between the growth in personal knowledge and developments in clinical expertise. It is the blend of personal knowledge along with other types of knowledge—empirical, ethical and aesthetic—which enables healthcare professionals to behave in a safe and accountable way.

So far we have been talking about individuals as 'authorities'. There is also 'group authority', perhaps most conventionally and historically seen and exercised through NHS Executive Groups, the Royal Colleges, the NMC, the Department of Health, and so on.

The 'new kids on the block' in this category may well be, for example, the National Institute for Health and Clinical Excellence (NICE) and the Commission for Health Improvement (CHI). Whilst we do not doubt either the power or wisdom of these 'outside' authorities in general, we wish to reiterate the point that reflective practitioners have the skills and courage to assert the power and relevance of knowledge generated from within their own individual, group or team work. Reflective practitioners are generators of knowledge, not solely consumers of other people's knowledge.

Borrowing

Healthcare knowledge does not emanate from a single source. Such knowledge is borrowed from other fields and disciplines such as medicine, psychology, sociology, history, physiology, education, and so on. It is smart to borrow knowledge if the ways of knowing we have at our disposal are seen to be inadequate in resolving the healthcare problems at hand. It is not smart to borrow per se. It is smart to know where to borrow from and even wiser to know how to use this newly acquired knowledge. We can take something and apply it directly to our clinical action or we can modify and customize it to suit our local needs. But borrowing has a down side. Rafferty (1996) summarizes the complex problem in relation to nurses, thus (pp.7–8):

> *The cognitive strategies which nurses have adopted in order to obtain professional 'uplift' have been characterized by two main approaches; the 'assimilationist' and the 'separatist'. In the former, nurses learn the language of education and research used by the 'established' disciplines*

and articulate nursing problems through methods 'owned' by these disciplines. The latter, separatist strategy, involves creating and claiming a new language, one which reflects the cultural specificity of nursing — that is, its 'difference' and distance from other disciplines. These strategies are not unique to nurses; they are typical of many marginal groups struggling to establish their identity in an environment where they are parvenus. Nurses have utilized both these strategies in legitimizing their claims to knowledge and expertise. In doing so, they have... sought the proxy patronage of medicine and social science to authorize claims to specialized knowledge and to elaborate the academic basis of nursing expertise. Although nurses may have been passive recipients of knowledge and work 'passed down' by others, they have also attempted to take control of that knowledge through research and curriculum development... the rise of academic nursing has been accompanied by a series of dilemmas for nursing as a discipline. These derive from a crisis of authority experienced in the intellectual identity of nursing as an academic subject, a crisis that nursing shares with other disciplines periodically.

Trial and error

This is an important part of generating practical knowledge. The use of the word 'error' always makes people concerned, and rightly so.

The phrase is meant to capture something of the fluidity of clinical work and how safe practice is also responsive practice. In other words, we often make quite subtle and sometimes unconscious modifications to our work to meet particular circumstances. 'Trial and error' in itself can be a misleading phrase. It should always be coupled with reflection-on-action, learning and a commitment to improve practice. Way back in 1859, Florence Nightingale in her *Notes on Nursing* began to demonstrate the need for nurses to be reflective. Burns and Grove (1993) call it trial and error. Reflective practitioners would call it 'learning from experience and careful reflective inquiry'. Nightingale presages this present-day concern, thus:

The everyday management of a large ward let alone a hospital — the knowing what are the laws of life and death for men and what the laws of health for wards — are not these matters of sufficient importance and difficulty to require learning by experience and careful inquiry, just as much as any art? They do not come by inspiration to the lady disappointed in love nor to the poor workhouse drudge hard up for a livelihood.
(in Whittington and Boore 1988: 109)

Role modelling

We all learn from others. No matter how much we know, we can never claim to know it all! We learn from observation, active and empathic listening, by watching a demonstration, imitating the work of others, and so on. Role models could, for example, be mentors, preceptors, tutors, 'supervisors' or respected colleagues. In *Table 3.1* we have extended the idea of acquiring knowledge through 'role-modelling' and linked it to some aspects of reflective practice.

Table 3.1 The healthcare worker as learner (adapted from Tomasello et al 1996: 202)

The Learner	Becoming knowledgeable	Activities
1 Imitator	Acquisition of 'know how to' knowledge	Observation in clinical setting, imitation of a role model. Learning through practice-makes-perfect and permanent. Being shown.
2 Collector	Acquisition of 'know that' knowledge	Learning through lectures, worksheets, books. Knowing more through didactic exposure. Being told.
3 Discoverer	Knowledge is 'constructed' by reflection-on-practice	Discovery learning, student-centred learning, learning through journal writing, critical incident analysis, concept mapping and a range of other reflective activities
4 Collaborator	Knowledge is generated and critiqued through collaboration, co-working and discussion	Learning through the benefits of establishing and sustaining reflective teams

When we learn through 'imitation', looking, and learning from the looking, is vital. For example, an experienced clinician goes through a sequence in a demonstration and models the actions and behaviours. The imitator repeats what they see until they have mastered the sequence steps and can demonstrate the skills competently. When we are in 'collection' mode we are essentially learning more about a subject, issue or healthcare concern. For this knowledge to be worthwhile, it must be relevant to practice in some way. This does not mean that it is always directly applicable to the current practice agenda of the learner. Relevance might mean that it helps us to appreciate the complexity of something better and helps us to get things into perspective. We might put it in our 'locker', then recall and apply it to practice later. Imitation and collection are some key ingredients of the view of the nurse as a 'knowledgeable doer'. What is implied by the term 'discoverer' is an active rather than a passive healthcare professional-as-learner. This view begins to draw explicitly upon reflective practice. It is also supportive of the third principle of reflection which values the personal-practical knowledge generated by individuals. This view also suggests that through reflection we not only generate knowledge but also know how we have arrived at what we claim to know. The learner as 'collaborator' takes things one step further. It is congruent with our view that reflective practice should involve a public and discursive element. In other words, knowledge for safe and accountable clinical action is not just 'out there' but actively constructed, negotiated and constantly redefined through discussion and conversation in reflective teams. Each of these 'modes of learning' are not mutually exclusive. Sometimes it is good and necessary to imitate. At other times we have to be more of a 'discoverer'. Some of the influences on which mode we need to use are the demands of the task, our experience, our own and others' expectations of the desirable outcome and the clinical context or environment in which all of these are located.

A 'sixth' way?

A sixth way of acquiring knowledge is embraced by the third principle of reflective practice. This sixth way is through systematic, supported and rigorous reflection-on-practice which generates personal-practical knowledge. This is knowledge worth knowing!

Without a commitment to valuing learning from experience through reflection, the kinds of sensitivity, the implications for clinical procedures and protocols and the greater sense of 'control' over action, described below, may well be lost. We formally acknowledge our thanks to Robyn Richens for this example. Wound care is a special interest of hers.

What knowledge is worth knowing? An example of the sixth way

One entry describes a patient who has a slow healing sinus which we had been treating for several weeks with slow but positive results. This particular day, the Registrar had seen the patient, was concerned with an increase in exudate from the area and ordered TDS [three times daily] dressings, which the nurse had implemented. I felt annoyed at hearing this, questioning what is to be gained and why put the patient through the discomfort. Literature and my own experience confirm that daily dressings are sufficient. I approached the Registrar and explained the facts. His reasoning was the patient had mentioned the increased discharge so he felt he should be seen to change things! The patient was concerned that I was changing the doctor's orders.

However, after explaining my reasoning he was happy to continue. I also made the patient responsible for the care of his skin, frequent pad changes and cleaning of the surrounding skin to protect it from the exudate. Later when I wrote about this incident in my journal I was aware of several issues; no one (myself included) had given this patient an explanation of the principles of wound healing, nor had we allowed him the responsibility for some of his own care in this area. The nurse on the morning shift and the patient had both believed that the doctor knew best, and when I explained my reasons to the doctor he agreed and was willing to hand over responsibility. I had been irritated by the lack of control I had in the situation until I realized that I did have the ability to change things and feel I have now earned the doctor's respect.
(Richens 1995: 3)

Turning personal-practical knowledge into 'living theory'

It is wise to view all knowledge as 'uncertain'. It is not fixed, static and unable to be reviewed. Griffiths (1988) suggests three reasons for this:

1. All knowledge is open to critique from others who might hold alternative views. It is therefore unwise to think that we can create a stable, unchanging knowledge base for healthcare, particularly in a rapidly changing society.
2. All knowledge reflects the individual perspectives and 'positions' of those who generate it. When we try to understand and use knowledge it is important to appreciate that perspectives and positions change. For example (p.82):

... it is important not to allow the norm for all knowledge to be set using the perspective of white, middle-class, Protestant, straight, able-bodied males.

3. All knowledge is generated by people who hold certain ethical and political views, for example, over what might be the purposes and impact of this knowledge. If some kinds of knowledge are for the improvement of clinical practice, and there is no consensus over what constitutes improvement, or understanding of the motives of the generators of this knowledge, then the whole situation becomes an uncertain one.

Already in this book we have seen that there are different kinds of knowledge, generated in different ways, to serve a variety of purposes.

You might also have noticed, in these early chapters, that knowledge can be 'displayed' and written down using different languages, some more technical, personal, visual or 'academic' than others. Additionally, we are now saying that knowledge should also be viewed as uncertain, provisional, situated, and revisable. It is through the processes of reflection that we can come to appreciate these things. These attributes of 'uncertainty' make Whitehead's (1993) view of knowledge as 'living', a powerful and attractive one.

The main idea behind Whitehead's work, originally developed in the field of teacher education, is the way he encourages us to account for our own development through the creation of our own 'living educational theories'. Nothing could be more relevant to healthcare professionals today, and it also allows us to introduce the fourth principle of reflective practice, which is:

> **Principle 4: Reflective practice is about learning how to account positively for ourselves and our work**

Whilst not denying the value of other kinds of knowledge, Whitehead argues that theory should be in a living form, made up from the descriptions and explanations of our own work and professional development. In this way, this 'living' form of knowledge, or 'theory', both reflects and acknowledges the power of context in the generation of knowledge. Whitehead argues that the explanations we give in trying to make sense of our practice come about if we address in a serious, critical and creative manner, such questions as: 'How do I improve my practice here?' This kind of knowledge is 'living' because it is based on practice, as lived and experienced by healthcare professionals themselves.

Lomax et al (1996) illustrate this idea of a living form of knowledge with reference to educational management thus (p.16):

A living theory is one that is continuously created and recreated through the validated explanations that individual managers offer of their own practices as they pursue their educational goals. These explanations are stimulated by intentional, committed action that stems from practical concerns about managing, and are reached through the analysis of careful descriptions that depend on rigorous methods of data collection and analysis.

This view of 'living' theory is highly relevant to all in healthcare, and perfectly consistent with and supportive of the first four principles of reflective practice which we have described to you.

Theory as a kind of knowledge: What theory? Whose theory? and Does it matter?

All we can do here is to outline the main ideas and arguments, sufficient to provide a framework of understanding for the following chapters. (For a more elaborate explanation, see Ghaye et al 1996.)

Theory is knowledge of a particular kind. Just as there are different kinds of knowledge, so are there different kinds of theory. People use the word 'theory' in many different ways. Here, for example, are some of the more common word associations:

- theory and practice
- theory-practice gap
- theory as irrelevant
- theory of what?
- theory as something you read about in books
- theory as that stuff you learn about on courses
- theory — whose?
- theory applied to practice
- theory — ugh!

In healthcare there has been a long-standing belief in a theory-practice gap. Some see these gaps as troublesome, others as helpful. Where you stand on this perhaps depends upon your definition of 'theory'.

In a very useful paper by Carr (1986), we find four approaches to understanding theory. We have applied these to healthcare. They are:

1. A commonsense approach

This locates or 'grounds' theory in the commonsense understandings of clinicians. It is articulated from within the world of practice. It is refined, reconstructed and validated in the light of its practical consequences.

2. An applied science approach

Here theory has to conform to the standards of rigour, validity, and reliability as universality laid down by 'science'. Its generation assumes that our practice is always amenable to scientific methods of investigation.

3. A practical approach

This approach sees theory as nourishing practical clinical wisdom. It supports and informs clinical decisions. It can be used to justify our practice because it embraces a consideration for both the means and the ends of healthcare.

4. A critical approach

This sees theory as enabling us to better understand why our practice is the way it is. It takes into consideration how historical, social and political forces serve to liberate or constrain what we do. It has the potential to enlighten and empower. Safe and accountable clinical practice requires clinicians to appreciate that not only are they consumers of knowledge (that is, of other people's knowledge) but also that they are generators of knowledge (personally and collectively owned) and that theory is a particular kind of knowledge. Argyris and Schön (1992: 4–5) explain:

> *Theories are theories regardless of their origin; there are practical, common-sense theories as well as academic or scientific theories. A theory is not necessarily accepted, good or true.... Theories are vehicles for explanation, prediction or control.*

At this point we are able to establish the fifth principle of reflective practice, which is:

Principle 5: Reflective practice does not separate practice and theory

Reflective practitioners have a particular view of practice and theory. Through systematic and rigorous forms of reflection-on-practice (see *Chapter 5*), clinicians are enabled to construct meaningful 'theories-of-action' which are in a 'living' form. They are living in the sense that they are made up of the essence of reflective conversations (see *Chapter 6*) which constitute descriptions, explanations and justifications of practice. Reflective conversations are public activities. They represent a public validation of practice. Linking practice with theory, through a reflective conversation, is a creative process. Carr (1986: 165) adds further clarification to our suggestion:

> *... all practice presupposes a more or less coherent set of assumptions and beliefs. It is, to this extent, always guided by a framework of theory. Thus, on this view, all practice, like all observations, is 'theory-laden'. Practice is not opposed to theory, but is itself governed by an implicit theoretical framework which structures and guides the activities of those engaged in practical pursuits.*

Principle 5 suggests that reflective practitioners do not separate practice from theory. They view clinical action (or practice) as theory-laden.

These theories guide and help to explain what they do. They are sometimes 'tacit'. One function of a reflective conversation is to make them more explicit and therefore more known, more open to critique and improvement. Clinical work reflects the personal theories which we hold. Practice, then, constitutes our 'theories-in-use' (Argyris and Schön 1992). Practice interacts with theory; they need each other. Through reflection-on-practice we generate 'practical theory'.

Reflection on practical theory, in turn, helps to inform and transform our clinical work.

- *What theory?* — practical
- *Whose theory?* — clinicians' own theories
- *Does it matter?* — but of course; practice and theory need each other.

References

Argyris C, Schön D (1992) *Theory-in-Practice: increasing professional effectiveness.* Jossey Bass, San Francisco

Basford L, Slavin O (1995) *Theory and Practice of Nursing.* Campion Press, Edinburgh

Benner P (1984) *From Novice to Expert: excellence and power in clinical nursing practice.* Addison-Wesley, Menlo-Park

Benner P, Tanner C, Chesla C (1996) *Expertise in Nursing Practice: caring, clinical judgement and ethics.* Springer Publishing Co, New York

Boud D, Keogh R , Walker D (1998) *Reflection: Turning Experience into Learning.* Kogan

Page, London

Burns N, Grove S (1993) *The Practice of Nursing Research: conduct,critique and utilization*. Harcourt Brace, London

Burrows D (1994) The nurse teacher's role in the promotion of reflective practice. *Nurse Educ Today* **15**: 346–50

Carper B (1978) Fundamental Patterns of Knowing in Nursing. *Adv Nurs Sci* **1** (1): 13–23

Carr W (1986) What is an educational practice? *J Phil Educ* **21** (2): 177–86

Chinn P, Kramer M (1995) *Theory and Nursing: a systematic approach*. Mosby, St Louis

Christensen P, Kenney J (1995) *Nursing Process: application of conceptual models*. Mosby, St Louis

Department of Health (2008) *A High Quality Workforce; NHS next stage review*. Department of Health, London.

Foucault M (1980) *Power/Knowledge: Selected Interviews and Other Writings*. Harvester Wheatsheaf, London

Gartner A, Latham G, Merrit S (1996) *The Power of Narrative: transcending disciplines*. Royal Melbourne Institute of Technology University, ultiBASE publication, Melbourne

Ghaye T et al (1996) *Theory-Practice Relationships: Reconstructing Practice: Self-supported Learning Experiences for Healthcare Professionals*. Pentaxion Press, Newcastle-upon-Tyne

Ghaye T, Lillyman S (2006) *Learning Journals and Critical Incidents: Reflective Practice for Healthcare Professionals*.(2nd ed) Mark Allen Publishing, Salisbury

Griffiths, M (1998) *Educational Research for Social Justice: getting off the fence*. Open University Press, Milton Keynes

Heron J (1998) *The Role of Reflection in a co-operative inquiry*. in Boud D, Keogh R, Walker D Reflection: Turning Experience into Learning. Kogan Page, London

Jenks J (1993) The pattern of personal knowing in nurse clinical decision-making. *J Nurs Ed* **32** (9): 399–405

Johns C, Freshwater D (2005) *Transforming Nursing through Reflective Practice*.(2nd ed) Blackwell Science, Oxford

Lomax P, Whitehead J, Evans M (1996) *Contributing to an epistemology of quality management practice*. in Lomax P, ed. Quality Management in Education: Sustaining the Vision through Action Research. Routledge and Hyde Publications, London

Lyotard J F (1984) *The Post-modern Condition: a report on knowledge*. Manchester University Press, Manchester

Newell R (1994) Reflection: art, science or pseudo-science. *Nurse Ed Today* 14: 79–81

Palmer A, Burns S, Bulman C (1994) *Reflective Practice in Nursing: The Growth of the Reflective Practitioner*. Blackwell Science, Oxford

PolanyiM(1958) *Personal Knowledge*. Routledge and Kegan Paul, London

Rafferty A (1996) *The Politics of Nursing Knowledge*. Routledge, London

Richens R (1995) *Beginning Journeys ... Reflective Practice and Journalling, A Collection of Work, Volume 1*. Department of Nursing, Midwifery and Health Education, Christchurch Polytechnic, Christchurch, New Zealand

Rose H (1994) *Love, Power and Knowledge: towards a feminist transformation of the sciences*. Polity Press, Cambridge

Sternberg R, Horvath J (1999) *Tacit Knowledge in Professional Practice: Researcher and Practitioner Perspectives*. Lawrence Erlbaum Associates, Mahwah, New Jersey

Tomasello M, Kruger A, Ratner H (1996) Cultural Learning. *Behavioural and Brain Sciences* **16** (3): 495–511

White J (1995) Patterns of knowing: review, critique and update. *Adv Nurs Sci* **17**(4): 73–86

Whitehead J (1993) *The Growth of Educational Knowledge: Creating your own Living Educational Theories*. Hyde Publications, Bournemouth

Whittington D, Boore J (1988) *Competence in Nursing*. in Ellis R, ed. Professional Competence and Quality Assurance in the Caring Professions. Chapman and Hall, London

Yaxley B (1991) *Developing Teachers' Theories of Teaching: a touchstone approach*. The Falmer Press, London

CHAPTER 4

Reflections on Schön: Fashion victims or joining up practice with theory?

Clearing some of the ground

We need to clear some ground first so that we can explain the essence of Schön's ideas about the reflective practitioner later in the chapter. To clear some ground we need to begin to look at some of the different (and everyday) views of reflection and reflective practice (Bright 1995). As we said earlier, we need to reject the idea that there is one sole meaning implied by the term reflective practice. This, of course, poses a problem for those who like to be told, 'Well, this is what reflective practice means, then'. The term cannot be defined in a sentence. The flip side of multiple meanings is well put by Morrison:

> *The notion of reflective practice has lost the sharpness of meaning since becoming popularized in the last 10 years. It has become unclear what constitutes reflective practice.*
> (Morrison 1995: 82)

It is the intention of this chapter to describe some of the different ways in which we can think about reflective practice.

'Everyday' reflective practice

We took the spirit of one view of reflection, described by Hall (1997) and, at the start of a reflective practice 'study day' at University College Worcester, asked a group of 15 practice nurses what they thought reflective practice meant to them. Here are some of their responses:

- navel gazing
- learning from the day's work
- reasoning

over and over things, round and round
honest with yourself

- questioning what you do
- being more aware
- thinking more deeply about things
- looking back over your shoulder
- justifying what you do
- making more sense of practice
- getting better at things,
- doing what I know and knowing why I do it.

It is obvious from these responses that there are many views about what reflection is and what reflective practitioners do. These responses also hint at the impact of reflection on the quality of care (Haddock 1997). In describing this view of 'everyday' reflective practice, Hall (1997) says that it, 'just happens' and it (p.2):

... is commonly referred to as 'what we do anyway'. Other people speak of everyday reflective practice as a solitary and tacit activity. One example of this is the notion of navel gazing (which has connotations of being a self-indulgent and time-wasting activity).

Hall goes on and quotes some of the participants from a reflective practice workshop which she attended. For example (p.2):

I am reflective, but I am not systematic. I don't really write it down. I just worry. A... possibly more fruitful everyday interpretation of reflective practice is that of creative daydreaming. Another workshop participant described this as,... 'when ideas pop up in the shower or at those times when I arrive home in my car and wonder how I got there'.

At one extreme, one of the founding fathers of reflection, John Dewey, describes reflection as a whole way of being; a disposition towards practice; a whole approach to the job (Dewey 1933). Others describe reflection more specifically, for example:

... as an intentional act of examining the rationale and justification of an action or belief.
(Tsang 1998: 23)

Some describe reflection in other ways:

- as a crucial element in the growth of professional people (Calderhead and Gates 1993)
- as a reaction against the view of professionals as 'technicians' who merely carry out what others, removed from practice, want them to do (Zeichner and Listen, 1996)
- as:

a generic term for those intellectual and affective activities in which individuals engage to explore their experiences in order to lead to new understandings and appreciations. It may take place in isolation or in association with others. It can be done well or badly, successfully or unsuccessfully.
(Boud et al 1998: 19)

and the reflective practitioner as:

... one who, given particular circumstances, is able to distance herself from the world in which she is an everyday participant and open herself to influence by others, believing that this distancing is an essential first step towards improvement.
(Day 1999: 218)

Reflection can therefore be about many things. It can be developed in different ways and serve many interests. It can serve a personal or a collective interest. It can be about personal growth which arises from 'self-study', and it can also be used to develop more effective healthcare teams and enhance organizational development. There are, then, many faces of reflection. For some it can have a rather soft, warm or 'touchy-feely' face, a bland, pappy and very 'subjective' face. For others, reflection has a more political, militant and critical edge — this is where certain types of reflection actively seek to improve things by challenging the status quo, routine and habitual practices. It is where it is used to question practice and those social and political forces which constrain and stifle what we do, or feel we should do. If one of the interests which reflection serves is of improving practice, then it must also display a creative face (Ghaye and Lillyman 2006).

Reflection and a sense of soul

The view of reflective practice as being about 'self' opens up some interesting ideas. In everyday thinking, this is reflection aligned to self-study; it can help to make us more self-aware and self-conscious (in a positive way), and more in touch with the many sides of our personalities or multiple selves (Harré, 1998). It can be about self-esteem, self-concept and self-development. In healthcare we work with both head and heart. We must feelingly know what is the most appropriate way to care. We are not machines. We have feelings.

When trying to develop reflective teams (and organizations) reflection-on-practice can help to provide a 'sense of soul to our work' (Hall 1997). It can help to bring everything together into a meaningful whole. An essential element of this 'sense of soul' would be reflective action (at individual, team and organizational levels) based on:

- **Authenticity**: coming to know our authentic self through meaningful relationships with others in our healthcare team and organization.
- **Intentionality**: where our shared intentions are to act in a systematic, supportive, constructively critical and creative manner in order to enhance practice and the quality of care. This refers to putting our 'heart and soul' into realizing our hopes.
- **Sensibility**: reflective practitioners are sensitive to their own needs and wants and to the needs and wants of those they work with and care for; reflection heightens our sensitivities.
- **Spirituality**: reflection can foster a deep sense of obligation, commitment and moral purpose to our work. Through our caring practices, we appreciate a sense of connectedness and mutual interdependence with those for whom we care. Through reflection we experience a sense of being part of and connected to something larger and more significant than 'the self'.

There is a clear 'sense of soul', in the way we are describing it, in the account of the practice of Brian Rushton and the South West Wirral Elderly Mental Health (EMH) community team (Rushton 1999). We believe that the 'sense of soul' in their work comes from the team's commitment to reflect on their practice. They use the Burford nursing development unit model (Johns, 1994). This 'sense of soul' is given life and colour in what they call their team philosophy, outlined below. (We thank Brian, Sue L, Helen, Neal, Claire, Rosemary, Sue V, Joan and Diane for their permission to use their work.)

We believe it is the right of all to be treated as an individual with honesty and respect in a non-discriminatory and non-judgemental way. We

value the right of each person to have their views heard and received with empathy, recognizing their cultural and spiritual beliefs with equal fairness. Communication should be effective and appropriate, providing education and positive support, networking with other agencies. All approaches will be of a therapeutic nature with the aim of enablement toward full potential, giving the right of the individual to choose their own plan of care — within the bounds of legislation. We believe in our team which will provide healthcare using a total teamwork approach.
(Rushton 1999: 277)

Fuzzy practice by fuzzy professions in a fuzzy world

Fuzzy thinking began to establish itself in the 1920s as a way of trying to come to terms with an increasingly complex world.

Traditional Western approaches... tend to be rooted in Aristotelian binary logic, where world is divided into good and bad, right and wrong, truth and lies, black and white, life and death, 0 and 1 and so on. This principle... has encouraged us to perceive our world, and our place in it, as one where clarity of decision-making is premised upon the clarity of our perspective.
(Grint 1997: 10)

So, how far does this kind of 'logic' fit with your world of clinical practice? Perhaps at times you have to work within a world of dualism — for example, the patient has or has not received the correct drugs; a bed is available or it is not; we are competent to practice or we are not; the decision to send the patient home is the right and not the wrong one; the bruised and lacerated female in a relationship with an alcohol-dependent partner is telling the truth and not lies. Sometimes we work within the world of dualism because the world would be too complicated to cope with in any other way.

But the world of practice is complicated! We cannot always rationalise away a practice world full of paradox, chance events, luck, accidents, subjectivity and Sod's Law. Sometimes we try to imagine away this fuzzy practice world by trying to impose certainty upon it, thus attempting to make it easier to understand and work within. Healthcare is an uncertain world in which the only thing that is certain is that nothing is certain. We can never be certain that things will go the same way again. There are just too many variables. The patients, their current condition, their history and hopes, the context of care, the treatment currently available, these are but a few of the influences which make practice an uncertain business. The world is fuzzy, and what we might usefully consider are ways of making this fuzziness more understandable, more malleable and less threatening (Rolfe 1997). Put another way, we need to make sense of the fuzziness. Reflective practice offers us this kind of hope. This prepares the way for the sixth principle of reflective practice, which is:

> **Principle 6: Reflective practice can help us make sense of our thoughts and actions**

If the world of healthcare itself is not predictable and stable, then we need some means of understanding what does, should or might work to good effect. In the short term — for example during a late Saturday shift in an accident and emergency department — anything can happen, but in the longer term, patterns do emerge and are discernable. Recognizing these patterns enables the department to plan and to operate efficiently and effectively, given the resources available. We make sense of the apparent chaos of the moment by reflecting on practice. Reflective practitioners see the fuzziness and the chaos as opportunities to learn. Reflection, as a way of making sense of uncertainty, can therefore become a constructive experience. The boundary between chaos and order becomes the leading edge for learning. Simply put, if we do not perceive the world to be fuzzy and chaotic, then there is no learning. No learning, then no improvement of practice.

Reflection and chaos: working at the boundary of stability and disorder

Something triggers reflection. We are arguing that 'fuzzy pictures' and 'apparent chaos' are two such triggers (for others, see *Chapter 8*). Chaos theory (Gleick 1987, Stewart 1989, Stewart and Golubitsky 1992, Field and Golubitsky 1992) offers reflective practitioners some very practical ways of trying to make sense of the uncertainty in their clinical worlds. It also provides some clues as to where to look to make more sense of the turbulence and patterns which arise as we manage care, often at the edge of order and chaos.

Reflection and searching for patterns

Stewart (1995) and Hardy and Redfem (1996) have crystallized in our minds a fundamental reason why we should engage in reflective practice.

In a very important sense, reflection represents an attempt to discover, make sense of and then perhaps to improve existing patterns and order. Chaos theory reminds clinicians that patterns actually exist where and when we thought the 'world' was messy and formless. Chaos is not complicated, unpatterned action; it is more subtle than this. Stewart (1995) argues that chaos is 'apparently' complicated; 'apparently' unpatterned behaviour. If the right lenses are used to see, then the patterns and hidden rhythms become discernible. It is at this point that we can begin to do something with them. The different types of reflection offer different lenses (Boykin 1998) with which to search for this pattern and order. Reflective practice also helps us to ask questions about the patterns we observe. These questions are to do with how and why the clinical patterns exist, how they have come to be this way and how we might influence and shape them. We should not forget that we live in a universe of patterns:

> *Every night the stars move in circles across the sky. The seasons cycle at yearly intervals. No two snowflakes are exactly the same, but they all have a sixfold symmetry. Tigers and zebras are covered in patterns of stripes, leopards and hyenas are covered in patterns of spots. Intricate trains of waves march across the oceans; very similar trains of sand dunes march across the desert. Coloured arcs of light adorn the sky in the form of rainbows, and a bright circular halo sometimes surrounds the moon on winter nights... Patterns possess utility as well as beauty. Once we have learned to recognise a background pattern, exceptions suddenly stand out. The desert stands still but the lion moves.*
> *(Stewart 1995: 1–3)*

Reflection helps us to recognise and make sense of the patterns in our work.

Reflection as breaking symmetry

There is something attractive about symmetry. Perhaps it is its repetitiveness, and therefore its predictability, which attracts us. Some healthcare professionals welcome, and actively seek, the appeal of practice-as-symmetry. We have repetitive clinical routines with drug rounds, handovers and the like. We can wrap ourselves up in these. They often become what is called our taken-for-granted clinical practice. They can act as a comfort blanket, offering a sense of security which comes from knowing what is likely to come, and is needed to be done, next.

The most important kinds of symmetry are called 'flips', 'turns' and 'slides'. These can be related to ways of reflecting on practice. For example, we often talk about flipping things over to try to understand the clinical incident another way. We flip things over in order to see the other side of the same thing. Rotation, or 'turning', is that kind of symmetry which is to do with rotating objects around a fixed point, like a wheel turning around its hub. In guided and structured reflection-on-practice we often turn things around. We consider a variety of points of view on the same thing. 'Slides', or translations, are a particular type of symmetry where transformations occur when an object or objects are slid along without rotating them. Slides can incorporate both horizontal and vertical movements. It is a way of moving things around, like pieces of a jigsaw. This, again, is helpful when reflecting on practice. As we slide one piece of the clinical jigsaw around, we not only align it with another to add meaning to it, but we leave a space behind, allowing either for further reflection, or for other pieces of practice to move into. Such a repositioning creates new pictures of clinical practice. All this is done within a fixed frame, too — the clinical context in which practice is embedded. The particular 'picture' is bounded. Flips, turns and slides can be viewed as useful reflective thinking strategies or, with a skilful facilitator, can become meaningful practical, art-based activities.

Breaking symmetry is another reflective process. This occurs when existing patterns are disturbed. Something acts as a catalyst to bring this about. For example, we might initiate it ourselves by asking ourselves searching questions about what we do. Having to make sense of a 'fuzzy picture', a moment of surprise, worry, excitement or concern, can also trigger this. An imposed change which requires new work habits, relationships or roles could also break the symmetry of existing practice, and those aspects of practice where personal values collide with organizational ones could do the same. Resistance to change is a good example in which symmetries of practice break reluctantly. When we break an existing symmetry of practice, rather a lot of it often survives. It is still present, in the 'system', somewhere and in some form! Memories of 'what it was like to work on this ward', of 'how things were around here', old habits and ways of working which cannot easily be unlearned, are all examples of fragments of former symmetries of practice.

We should learn from both the symmetry and the broken symmetry of practice. In doing so, we may experience feelings of vulnerability and threat. Participating in reflective teams can help individuals to work through these productively. We should reflect on the point made by Briggs (1992) when he suggests that an extremely fertile area on which to focus our attention if we wish to improve what we do is (p.21):

... the ferociously active frontier that has been found to exist between stability and incomprehensible disorder.

Reflections on Schön

Donald Schön has made an enormous contribution to our understanding of reflective practice (Schön 1983, 1987, 1991). He has fuelled debate in such a way that healthcare work embracing and living out the 'R word' appears to continue to gain ground. NHS Trusts with aspirations to 'invest in people' or to become 'learning organizations' (see *Chapter 10*), and recent Government initiatives concerning clinical governance and particularly clinical supervision have, for example, stoked up the fire. So what, in essence, did Schön say to make him so popular? Why do his ideas command such interest and influence? There are three main reasons for this state of affairs. Schön disliked the dominant and prevailing way in which knowledge about and for practice was conceived. He mistrusted and disliked the way three things were being separated — he called them 'dichotomies'. In particular, the dichotomies were:

1. The way means were being separated from ends.
2. The way research was separated from practice.
3. The separation of knowing from doing.

Schön not only argued against these three things but, in doing so, emphasized that we should recognize the importance of 'practical knowledge' (our Principle 3). He disliked these three dichotomies so much that he said we should look for an alternative 'epistemology of practice'. In other words, that we should think about the way we generate and value knowledge in a very different way (Schön 1971).

Schön and his dislike of technical rationality

Schön's work contains a critique of something called 'technical rationality'. This is linked to the idea of practice being separated from theory, and of the 'worker' (such as the nurse, midwife, health visitor, therapist, social worker or teacher) being seen as a 'technician' who almost unthinkingly applies other people's knowledge to his or her own practice. Schön argued that the 'technical-rational' ways of viewing the links between the generation of knowledge and professional practice were (and still are?) dominant. Briefly, this means that knowledge is generated in such organizations of higher education as universities and research centres. This knowledge is 'theoretical' and is about how to achieve certain 'ends'. Hospitals, homes which care for the elderly, units, wards, departments, surgeries, walk-in clinics and the like are worlds of practice. In this technical-rational mode of thinking, the healthcare workers' task is viewed as applying the theoretical knowledge from the universities or the 'academy', in order to solve their practical problems. It is an application of theory to practice, and it devalues the knowledge which clinicians, for example, develop about and through their work. Clinicians are viewed as 'technicians' because they never question the values which underpin their practice and make them the kind of healthcare professionals which they are. They rarely question the context in which they are working, and how this liberates or constrains what they do.

There are some very real problems incurred with holding this technical-rational view. Firstly, the ends or products of healthcare work are rarely fixed. They are often contested. People have different views about them. This is pervasive in the 'educare' professions such as nursing, social work, teaching, and so on. Take any 'end' that you can think of — it does not have to be clinical in kind, it could be managerial or professional — and then reflect on this point. Clinical supervision is one example. The 'ends' (as well as the means) are contested. Are the ends to 'make individuals feel better', 'to remedy clinical deficits', 'to provide management with a stick', or 'to help to foster a learning culture within the organization', and so on. Secondly, we need to question the usefulness and relevance of knowledge which is produced out of the context to which it is to be applied. We have to ask questions about who is generating this knowledge for practitioners, and what exactly their motives are. This separation of the knowledge 'producers' from the 'consumers' is seen by some as divisive and elitist. Hooks (1995), for example, holds the following view of the situation (p.64):

... the uses these individuals (i.e. academics) make of theory is instrumental. They use it to set up unnecessary and competing hierarchies of thought which re-inscribe the politics of domination by designing work as either inferior, superior, or more or less worthy of attention... And it is easy to imagine different locations, spaces outside academic exchange, where such theory would not only be seen as useless, but as politically non-progressive, a kind of narcissistic, self-indulgent practice that at most seeks to create a gap between theory and practice so as to perpetuate class elitism.

This is a powerful message and gives us much food for thought. It links with what we were saying in *Chapter 3*. In a seminar at Worcester, with an experienced group of clinical nurse specialists, we debated this view put forward by Hooks. Some of the issues we needed to reflect upon were that much of the 'theoretical' knowledge which the group had come to know in the past:

- had, and still was, being generated by those in the 'academy' who wished to 'mystify' the knowledge generation business and so exclude distance, divide and separate themselves from those 'in practice'
- was generated in order to silence or devalue the voice of the practitioner and someone able to generate their own practical theories
- could be used as an instrument of domination; it was about one kind of knowledge being more worthy than other kinds
- created an oppressive hierarchy in which theoretical knowledge is viewed as being more important than practical knowledge.

A third difficulty with holding the technical-rational view is that the assumption that the problems of everyday clinical practice can always be solved by applying someone else's knowledge to one's own practice, is simplistic. It devalues the art and skilfulness of the healthcare professional caring for particular patients in particular circumstances. Our everyday 'problems' are not simply pre-defined, but are constructed through our engagement with the 'indeterminate zone of practice' which, typically, is characterized by 'uncertainty, uniqueness and value conflict' (Schön 1987: 6).

In this scenario, what are we to do when we find that, in trying to apply theory to practice, the theory fails to solve our immediate, local and particular care problem? What happens when the theory fails to explain our practice to us and to others? In the busy, fuzzy and often chaotic worlds of clinical practice, 'problems' are many and varied, often difficult to define and sometimes to resolve. They cannot always be solved by the application of someone else's theoretical knowledge. Schön turns this technical-rational view around and talks about how reflection helps us to 'frame' and 're-frame' problems; how we should value and use the kind of knowledge which is embedded in our workplaces, generated by our practice and shared amongst practitioners themselves. This set of issues is beautifully summed up by Gould (1996: 2-3):

> *A not uncommon illustration of this might be a duty social worker, called to the police station to assess someone arrested for a breach of the peace because the arresting officer thinks the person may be suffering from a mental disorder. Whether the professional social work issues raised by this situation relate primarily to criminality, a mental health crisis or some other problem still to be discovered such as homelessness, is not pre-determined at the point of referral, but is negotiated via a complex series of transactions between the worker, the detained individual and possibly other actors such as police or psychiatrists.*

From this perspective, the kind of 'theoretical' knowledge we have been describing is not a neutral, value-free resource (Gould 1996: 2–3)

> *... which can be drawn down and directly applied, but... only of use when mediated through the complex filters of practice experience. In order to become a tool for practice, the practitioner has to transform theory in the light of learning from past experience (reflection-on-action).*

Schön and joining up practice with theory

There are three elements in Schön's idea of practical knowledge. These are represented in *Figure 4.1*, and are 'knowing-in-action', 'reflection-in-action' and 'reflection-on-practice' (we emphasize the latter in this book). To these three we have added 'meta-reflection', or thinking again about all our previous reflections. We have also shown the link between Argyris and Schön's (1992) idea of a 'theory-of-action' and 'knowing-in-action'.

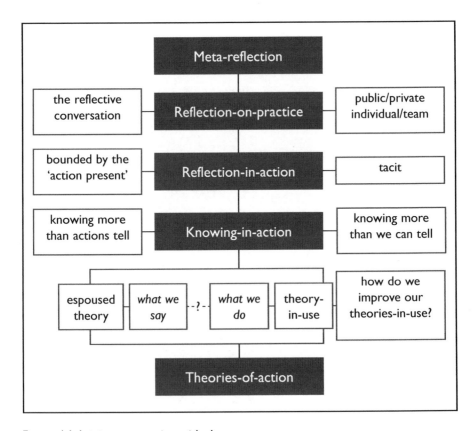

Figure 4.1: Joining up practice with theory.

Knowing-in-action linked to theories-of-action

The essence of this element, in Schön's view of practical knowledge, is that what we know shows in what we do. There are two parts to this. The first is that in trying to improve practice we have to begin by reflecting on what we actually do. This reflection generates a rich and detailed knowledge base. The second part is that this knowledge is drawn upon by us in our caring work. It then becomes our 'knowing-in-action'. Much of this knowing is often difficult to make explicit, to name and talk about. Schön (1992) called it 'intuition' and 'instinct'.

This view of knowing-in-action is linked to an extremely different view of theory from that which we described earlier. It is a view which acknowledges that we develop our own theories — 'customized' and 'tailored' ones — which help to guide and explain what we do. We have 'theories' about appropriate care management, about the best use of limited resources, about effective leadership, about communicating meaningfully, and so on. Making this kind of theory explicit, that is putting words to it and discussing it, is an important function of reflection. Schön develops this idea in his work with Argyris (1992). They pull all of these thoughts together into their view of a 'theory-of-action'. This is a highly relevant collection of ideas and, again, comes in two parts (see *Figure 4.1*) — our 'espoused' theories and our 'theories-in-use'. The former is what we say or claim we do, or want to do. The latter is about what actually happens in practice (note the link here with knowing-in-action). Normally we can find out what these theories-in-use are if we observe a colleague at work. Reflection provides the basis for improvement of our theories-in-use. We have a problem, though, if we cannot articulate what these theories are. Argyris and Schön (1992) make the point (p.10):

> *How can we change an existing theory-in-use or learn a new theory-in-use when we cannot state what is to be changed or learned?*

Hence the link, shown in *Figure 4.1*, between these theories and reflection-on-practice.

Reflection-in-action

When our 'knowing-in-action' produces an unexpected outcome or a surprise, one of two types of reflection can then follow (see also 'Reflection-on-practice', overleaf). The first is reflection-in-action, which occurs during (but without interrupting) our caring work. It is thinking about how to reshape (and adjust) what we are doing whilst it is under way. Schön argued that it is central to the art by which professionals handle and resolve their difficulties and concerns about practice, whilst actually in practice. Essentially, it is about thinking in the midst of action. It is thinking about doing something whilst actually doing it; thinking about what to say to a patient whilst saying it; thinking about handling a conflict situation, such as needing to admit a patient on to the ward when there is no bed available, whilst trying to resolve it. It is not about 'stopping and thinking' in the midst of action. It is about being 'on the spot' and 'thinking on your feet'. Reflection-in-action is a very elusive and puzzling phenomenon. It is also difficult because care is dynamic and ever-changing. At each moment, something situation-specific is happening. We do not know much about it. More healthcare research is needed to understand it better.

Reflection-in-action generates a kind of knowledge on which we depend in order to perform our tasks spontaneously. It tells us something about the adequacy of our 'knowing-in-action' and it guides further action. Eraut (1995) looks at this in some detail and, in particular, at how reflection needs to be understood in relation to 'time' (that is, when it occurs) and the context (the clinical situation in which we find ourselves) in which it occurs.

Reflection-on-practice

This is the second kind of reflection. It is the main focus of this book and others in the series. It is usually taken to mean reflection after the event. It can also include reflecting on some aspect of care before the event, but this is a less common expression of it. It is a way we can come to know our 'tacit' knowledge. Reflection-on-practice can be practised individually or in group situations. It can be a private, solitary, introspective activity, or a more public, discursive, team-type activity. There are numerous ways to facilitate this kind of reflection, for example journal writing and critical incident analysis, and these are reviewed in Ghaye and Lillyman (2006). Clinical supervision is based upon the idea of reflection-on-practice. The literature evidences other ways, such as using concept mapping, drama and role play, shared-critical reading groups, story-telling, conversational analyses (see *Chapter 5*), visual art, poetry, music and combinations of all of these, and more.

Meta-reflection

Meta-reflection is thinking again about our reflections-on-practice. It is stepping back and checking out what we thought and said earlier. It is further removed from the action than reflection-on-practice, and certainly from reflection-in-action. It really comes into its own in the context of triadic reflective arrangements (say in the context of clinical supervision) and reflective teams. Skilled facilitators, or critical friends, are usually a very important part of encouraging meta-reflection. Like reflection-on-practice, meta-reflection should be seen as an integral part of the learning process, not just something else bolted on from time to time. We discuss meta-reflection in the next chapter in the context of developing and sustaining reflective conversations.

Some other types of reflection

There are many other kinds, sequences and levels of reflection. These are presented in various 'models' which serve different purposes and interests, and which start and take the learner through certain reflective processes in different ways. These are critically reviewed in Ghaye and Lillyman (2006). Some models are more or less *'cyclical'*, thus emphasizing the continuous nature of learning through reflection. Some are more or less *'flexible'*. Some appear to drag the learner rather mechanistically through a series of steps, stages or questioning strategies, while others respect the fact that we do not all start to reflect from the same point. For some, reflection might begin with some frustrating or surprising aspect of care. Some might be reflecting on something new which was tried with a patient and which went particularly well. For others, reflection may begin with a mismatch between what is felt to be needed to improve the quality of care and what can be achieved, and so on. Another good thing about flexible models is that they are responsive to the way in which we learn. Improving care neither proceeds in a fixed and sequential way, nor in the same way for all of us. For example, we might choose to reflect on an aspect of our own practice first, and learn from that. Alternatively, we might think it appropriate to reflect on the way we do things, as a team. It might be that it is better to start with a more 'global' view of practice by reflecting on the general context of it. This would include thinking about the relationships between individuals and departments outside, but linked to where we work, for example, in-patient with out-patient departments, accident and emergency with various admission wards, medical with surgical directorates, hospital with GP surgeries, primary with secondary care groups, nursing with other professions allied to medicine, healthcare with education, and so on. What we reflect upon, and the order of our reflection, will vary between individuals and groups.

Other models are more or less *'focused'*. This is needed to enable meaningful learning to take place. Some of us need to be kept more focused, others like more flexibility to explore, or even to 'slosh around' for a while! Flexibility and focus are related to the four important ideas of guidance, structure, support and challenge in reflection.

Finally, there are some models which are more or less *'holistic'* in nature. These models serve to remind us that we do not work in a vacuum but in a social and political context. They link personal and professional values with practice; healthcare intentions with actions; individual with team development, and all within a clinical context which oscillates at the boundary between stability and chaos.

Day (1999) offers us an extremely helpful summary of some of the important ideas we have presented in this chapter (see *Table 4.1*). We have modified it slightly to be more appropriate to healthcare.

Reflective practitioners as fashion victims?

Both the word 'reflection', and exhortations to become reflective practitioners, appear to continue to gain ground in healthcare. It is dangerous to become swept along in any tide of events, swimming with the current, just accepting what is happening. It is dangerous to receive others' 'wisdom' unquestioningly. We should be able to make up our own minds about the value of a thing. We should not be afraid to speak out; to 'go against the flow'; to ask for evidence rather than blindly accepting 'reality' as described by others (Newman 1999).

Reflection continues to become a feature of healthcare and organizational development. More and more resources are being devoted to its promotion (see *Empowerment Through Reflection: The narratives of healthcare professionals*, edited by Ghaye, Gillespie and Lillyman 2000, in this series) and there are many claims being made for its use (Clarke, James and Kelly 1996). James and Clarke (1994) summarize some of these with regard to nursing, thus:

- Reflection is an integral part of experiential learning and the development of practical knowledge.
- Reflection will lead to better practice.
- Reflective practice is necessary for effective nursing.
- Reflective practice will bring universal benefits.
- All nurses can be reflective practitioners.
- Reflective practice models enhance professional status.
- Reflective practice values each nurse's professional knowledge.

Table 4.1 Types of reflection related to concerns and contexts (after Day 1999). No hierarchy is implied here.

REFLECTION TYPE	NATURE OF REFLECTION	POSSIBLE CONTEXT
Reflection-in-action	**Contextualization of multiple viewpoints:** Drawing on any of the possibilities below applied to situations as they are actually taking place.	Dealing with on-the-spot professional problems as they arise (thinking can be recalled and then shared with others later).
Reflection-on-action	**Interpersonal:** Recognizing the self as contributing to social action; examining one's own behaviour in the context of personal values and emotions.	Thinking about the effects of one's own biography and feelings upon the management of care.
	Critical: (Social reconstructions) Seeing as problematic, according to ethical criteria, the goals and practices of one's profession.	Thinking about the effects upon others of one's actions, taking account of social, political and/or cultural forces.
	Dialogue: (Deliberative, cognitive, narrative) Weighing competing claims and viewpoints, and then exploring alternative solutions.	Hearing one's own voice (alone, or with another) exploring alternative ways to solve problems in a broader healthcare context.
	Descriptive: (Social efficiency, developmental, personalistic) Seeking what is seen-as 'best possible' practice.	Analysing one's performance in the clinical professional role (probably alone), exploring reasons for actions taken.
Technical Rationality	**Technical:** (Decision-making about immediate behaviours or skills) Drawn from a given research/theory base, but always interpreted in the light or personal worries, previous experience and employer expectations.	Examining one's use of essential knowledge and clinical skills in a defined context in relation to results-driven demands.

In the spirit of reflection, we suggest that it is right and proper to think carefully about the claims being made for reflective practice. Totterdell and Lambert (1999) offer us some useful reflective questions, for example in relation to healthcare:

1. Can we say what this thing called 'reflective practice' is (can it be described or its impact felt)?
2. Can we specify when it happens (and under what conditions and within what time-frame)?
3. Can we be certain whether it can be taught/learned (and by whom) and what research evidence is there that it is effective?
4. Do we really know what it is for (is it, *inter alia,* a necessary condition for becoming a healthcare worker or a criterion for distinguishing professional from non-professional practice)?
5. Do we claim (or imply), or sound as if we claim, that reflective practice provides an epistemology for everyday clinical and professional healthcare practice?

We need to think carefully and critically about the nature and potency of reflective practice in healthcare, or we may well be accused of 'jumping upon (yet another) bandwagon'. We may simply be fashion victims (knowingly or otherwise). We would argue that Principle 6 (*Reflective practice can help us make sense of our thoughts and actions*) gives reflection bite and relevance in the contemporary condition of postmodernity. Postmodernism questions the certainties of the past. It overturns generalities and universal 'truths', celebrates the particular and the local and recognizes difference. It is:

... based on specific cultural contexts, on localized and particularized knowledge and the valuing of a multiplicity of experience.
(Usher and Edwards 1994)

The kinds of 'theoretical' knowledge we were describing earlier (universal, impersonal, general, and objective), which downgraded practical knowledge, is not so much rejected as no longer just taken on trust. Postmodern thinking now asks such questions as: 'Who generates this knowledge?', 'What power do they have?' and 'Who is being excluded as a consequence?'

Reflective practice opens up a healthy debate within and between us about the nature of our caring work, how it has come to be this way, what sustains and erodes it and what we can or might do to improve the situation. It also challenges those conventional (modernist) ways of generating and valuing knowledge. As we have said, this has disadvantaged and marginalized local and practical knowledge; it has devalued the personal and the particular. In doing so, it has disempowered and silenced many healthcare practitioners. Reflective practice, then, has a seventh principle. It is:

Principle 7: Reflective practice generates locally owned knowledge

References

Aldershot Grint K (1997) *Fuzzy Management: Contemporary ideas and practices at work.* Oxford University Press, Oxford Argyris C, Schön D (1992) *Theory in Practice: Increasing Professional Effectiveness.* Jossey Bass, San Francisco

Boud D, Keogh R, Walker D (1998) Promoting Reflection in Learning: A model, in Boud D, Keogh R, Walker D, eds Reflection: *Turning Experience into Learning.* Kogan Page, London

Boykin A (1998) Nursing as Caring through the Reflective Lens. in Johns C, Freshwater D *Transforming Nursing through Reflective Practice.* Blackwell Science, Oxford

Briggs J (1992) *Fractals: the patterns of chaos.* Thames and Hudson, London

Bright B (1995) What is reflective practice? *Curriculum* 16 (2): 69-81

Calderhead J, Gates P, eds (1993) *Conceptualising Reflection in Teacher Development.* The Falmer Press, London

Clarke B, James C, Kelly J (1996) Reflective Practice: reviewing the issues and refocussing the debate. *IntJNurs Stud*33 (2): 171-80

Day C (1999) Researching Teaching through Reflective Practice, in Loughran J, ed. *Researching Teaching: Methodologies and Practices for Understanding Pedagogy.* The Falmer Press, London

Dewey J (1933) *How We Think: A restatement of the relation of reflective thinking to the educative process.* Henry Regnery Publishers, Chicago

Eraut M (1995) Schön Shock: a case for refraining reflection-in-action. Teachers and *Teaching: Theory and Practice* 1 (I): 9—22

Field M, Golubitsky M (1992) *Symmetry in Chaos.* Oxford University Press, Oxford

Ghaye T, Lillyman S (2006) *Learning Journals and Critical Incidents: Reflective Practice for Healthcare Professionals. 2nd edition* Mark Allen Publishing, Salisbury

Gleick J (1987) *Chaos: making a new science.* Viking Penguin, New York

Gould N (1996) Introduction: social work education and the 'crisis of the professions', in Gould N, Taylor I, eds *Reflective Learning/or Social Work.* Ashgate Publishing Limited

Haddock J (1997) Nurses' perceptions of reflective practice. *Nurs Stand* 11(32): 39-tl

Hall S (1997) Forms of reflective teaching practice in higher education, in Pospisil R,

Willcoxson L, eds *Learning through Teaching*: 124-31, Proceeding of the 6th Annual Teaching Learning Forum, Murdoch University

Hardy P, Redfem L (1996) Threads of reflection and the patterns they weave. Paper presented at the conference: Transforming Nursing through Reflective Practice. Robinson College, Cambridge

Harré R (1998) *The Singular Self: An introduction to the psychology of personhood*. Sage Publications, London

Hooks B (1995) Teaching to Transgress: education as the practice of freedom. Routledge, London

James C, Clarke B (1994) Reflective Practice in nursing: issues and implications for nurse education. *Nurse Educ Today* **14**: 82—90

Johns C, ed. (1994) *The Burford NDU model*: caring in practice.Blackwell Science, Oxford

Morrison K (1995) Dewey, Habermas and reflective practice. *Curriculum* **16** (2): 82-94

Newman S (1999) Constructing and critiquing reflective practice. *Educational Action Res* **J7** (I): 145-61

Rolfe G (1997) Science, abduction and the fuzzy nurse: An exploration of expertise. *JAdv Nurs* **25**: 1070-5

Rushton B (1999) Pause for thought. *Mental Health Care* **2** (8): 277-9

Schön D (1971) Implementing programs of social and technological change. *Technological Review* **73** (4): 47-51

Schön D (1983) *The Reflective Practitioner: How professionals think in action*. Basic Books, New York

Schön D (1987) E*ducating the Reflective Practitioner: Towards a new design for teaching and learning in the professions*. Jossey Bass, San Francisco

Schön D, ed. (1991) *The Reflective Turn: Case Studies in and on Educational Practice*. Teacher's College Press, New York

Schön D (1992) The Theory of Inquiry: Dewey's legacy to education. *Curriculum Inquiry* **22**: 119—39

Stewart I (1989) *Does God play Dice?* Blackwell Publishing, Oxford

Stewart I (1995) *Nature's Numbers: discovering order and pattern in the universe*.

Weidenfield and Nicholson, London

Stewart I, Golubitsky M (1992) *Complexity: the emerging science at the edge of order and chaos*. Simon and Schuster, New York

Totterdell M, Lambert D (1999) The Professional Formation of Teachers: a case study in reconceptualising initial teacher education through an evolving model of partnership in training and learning. *Teacher Development* **2** (3): 351-71

Tsang N (1998) Re-examining reflection — a common issue of professional concern in social work, teacher and nurse education. *J Interprofessional Care* **12** (I): 21-31

Usher R, Edwards R (1994) *Postmodernism and education: different voices, different worlds*. Routledge, London

Zeichner K, Listen D (1996) *Reflective Teaching: An Introduction*. Lawrence Earlbaum Associates, New Jersey

CHAPTER 5

The reflective conversation: What reality? Whose reality?

As healthcare professionals we have many duties. Daily we may juggle clinical, professional, managerial and research roles. We also carry out many tasks which may be variously regarded as 'basic', 'routine', 'ordinary', 'extraordinary', 'special', 'enjoyable', and so on. In all of this, whether it is when washing an elderly patient, trying to explain to a student nurse that her manner is somewhat abrasive, trying to relate meaningfully to a patient suffering from a chronic form of dementia, breaking the news of a healthy new-born baby to an expectant family, and much, much more, we need to be particularly conscious of the power of language. When we are being the patient's advocate we are, in an important sense, enabling the patient to have a voice, enabling their thoughts, emotions, hopes and anxieties to find expression. Each one of us has a voice, although it may of course be expressed in very different ways. With this in mind we suggest that two fundamental skills of all healthcare professionals are: firstly to discover and reflect on their own voice and secondly to enable others to hear and claim their own. The process of reflection-on-practice is central to this. In the context of this chapter, the idea of voice finds expression and significance in a particular kind of dialogue which we will call 'a reflective conversation'. Its introduction allows us to present an eighth principle of reflective practice, which is (see Ghaye and Lillyman, 2007):

> Principle 8: The reflective conversation is at the heart of the process of reflecting-on-practice

Some purposes of conversations

When caring for others we spend much of our time talking. Some of this talk is conversational in kind; it is not private, 'talking-to-yourself'-type conversation, but a public meaning-making process, which we construct with others. Feldman (1999) suggests that conversations serve three purposes. These are:

1. Conversations help us to make decisions (p.134):

   Through talking, listening, questioning and reflecting, the conversation process allows the participants the opportunities to develop understanding that can then be used to support decisions about the choice of goals or actions. In this way, it can be seen that conversation aids in practical decision making....

   Through clinical conversations we can (but not always) come to a common, co-operative or collaborative decision.
2. Conversations enable us to exchange knowledge: In *Chapter 3* we spoke about three kinds of knowledge. Conversations serve the purpose of enabling us to generate and consume 'know-how-to' do something knowledge, 'know-that' and 'know-why'-type knowledge.
3. Conversations aid understanding: Through speaking, actively listening, reflecting and speaking again, we give ourselves opportunities to deepen our understanding about a particular practice incident. Understanding something better does not always end in agreement amongst the participants:

   ... it is important to think of each participant coming to an understanding through the conversation, rather than all the participants arriving at a common understanding.
   (Feldman 1999: 136)

A clinical conversation as a co-operative dialogue

Clinical conversations occur between and among people. They are related to the management of care — in other words, to practice. They involve a sharing of thoughts and feelings as well as of information relevant to the topic of the conversation. There should also be a shared intentionality to come to some richer understanding of the practice incident, which might then result in some kind of appropriate action (or non-action). Due to pressures on the time of clinical staff, the participants need to feel that the conversation has a direction; that it is going somewhere. Sometimes this is not possible. We may not always know what will come out of a conversation but we at least need to feel that it has the potential to move our thinking and/or practice forward in some way.

Developing and sustaining a reflective conversation (which we define below) is dependent upon its being seen as a co-operative dialogue. Senge (1992) makes an interesting distinction between 'discussion' and 'dialogue'. He describes a discussion as being like a game of ping-pong, where ideas are batted around, to and fro, with someone (or a group) 'winning'. A dialogue is not about trying to 'win' but about individuals gaining insights which they could not achieve on their own. The participants are not in opposition but co-operatively participating in the development of meanings. This is about seeing clinical practice more deeply, richly and holistically. These insights are themselves capable of constant development and improvement. Interestingly Senge (1992) says that, 'in dialogue people become observers of their own thinking'. This is a direct link to the way in which we described reflection 'in' and 'on' action in the previous chapter.

Co-operative clinical dialogues can only occur when we see each other as 'colleagues' who want to benefit from dialogue, and when we are respectful of each other's vulnerabilities and 'agendas'. With this in mind, such dialogues can be creative as the participants try to develop a richer grasp of complex care issues.

Some kinds of conversation

Feldman (1999) identifies three kinds of helpful conversation in the context of collaborative action research.

1. **Conversation as part of an 'oral inquiry process'**: Feldman quotes the work of Cochran-Smith and Lytle (1993) as an illustration of this. It is essentially an oral process. It is one where two or more people jointly research their experiences, build on each other's insights and solve problems. It is not simply 'talk', but a self-conscious and self-critical attempt to improve practice.
2. **Collaborative conversations**: The work of Hollingsworth (1994) illuminates this kind of conversation. The features are that these conversations go 'beyond pleasant and informative chats' and are focused on 'practice-based concerns'. The participants have to be willing to share, and to collaborate in trying to make more sense of practice.
3. **Long and serious conversations**: Feldman quotes his own work here and argues that this kind of conversation is part of 'enhanced normal practice' (Feldman 1996). This is comprised of three processes: anecdote-

telling, the trying out of ideas, and systematic inquiry. Long and serious conversations are at the heart of enhanced normal practice.

'A reflective conversation with a situation': The work of Schön

In the previous chapter, we discussed how Schön has made an important contribution to our understanding of reflective practice. Central to Schön's argument are ideas related to what we know, and how this 'knowing' is put into action. He argues that much of this knowing is hard to put into words (Schön 1987). The knowing is often described as unconscious and tacit (Polanyi 1958). It can, however, reveal itself in our actions — in other words, in what we do when caring for others. Schön describes a process of improvement whereby, quite literally through conversation, situations which are uncertain, unstable, unique and value-laden come to be known, better understood, handled and managed. The process is not unlike what might take place in some clinical supervision meetings. For example, after the initial presentation of the topic of conversation what Schön calls the 'framing of the problem', there is a

> *...web of moves, consequences, implications, appreciations and further moves ... some moves are resisted while others generate new phenomena.*
> (Schön 1983: 94)

Through this conversation with the situation, the participants have to 'listen to the situation's back-talk, forming new appreciations which guide further moves' (Schön 1983: 94). This is an interactive process of construction and reconstruction of meanings and actions. Schön called it 'framing and reframing' the problem. It is energized and made possible through a reflective conversation with a situation. But the process is not an easy one. In being open to the 'situation's back-talk', the participant (Schön 1983: 164):

> *...must be willing to enter into new confusions and uncertainties. Hence, he must adopt a kind of double vision. He must act in accordance with the view he has adopted, but he must recognise that he can always break it open later, indeed, must break it open later in order to make new sense of his transaction with the situation. This becomes more difficult to do as the process continues. His choices become more committing; his moves, more nearly irreversible. As the risk of uncertainty increases, so does the temptation to treat the view as the reality.*

The first message here is that improving our thinking and practice, and the context in which our healthcare work is embedded, needs to be seen as a continuous and lifelong learning process. The second message is more contentious: to say that as the process unfurls and the conversation develops, choices become more committing and irreversible is to devalue and deny the power which certain kinds of reflection and reflective practice have to guard against just this. In summary, then, Schön describes reflective practice as taking the form of a 'reflective conversation with the situation' between two people. He draws a clear distinction between the reflective practitioner and the client, with the former facilitating the conversation. The interaction between the two is conditioned by something called a 'reflective contract' where the two agree to

> *...inquire into the situation, for which the client seeks help; to try to understand what he is experiencing and to make that understanding accessible to the practitioner when he does not understand or agree... The practitioner agrees to deliver competent performance to the limits of his capacity; to help the client understand the meaning of the professional's advice and the rationale for his actions, while at the same time he tries to learn the meanings his actions have for his client; to make himself readily confrontable by his client; and to reflect on his own tacit understandings when he needs to do so in order to play his part in fulfilling the contract.*
> (Schön 1983: 297)

The notion of a reflective contract is, in essence, a helpful one, for instance in the context of clinical supervision, but it is not without its problems. Three questions now need to be raised. They are:

1. What is a reflective clinical conversation?
2. How far would I recognise one if I heard one?
3. How would I set about facilitating and nurturing a conversation of this kind?

We address these questions in the rest of this chapter.

Qualities of the reflective clinical conversation

A focus on caring values

This is a fundamental and defining quality. In our experience, it is the one with which we have most trouble. To be called a reflective conversation, there needs to be some consideration and questioning of the caring values to which the healthcare professionals are committed and which they try to live out in their work. Professional and personal values are those fundamentally important things which make healthcare professionals the kind of people they are. They give their caring work its shape, form and purpose. Coming to know them, justifying and living them out, is something to which it is worthy to aspire (see *Chapter 6*). None of this is easy, though. Even quite experienced practitioners have difficulty in articulating their values and in addressing those things which get in the way of putting values into practice (Ghaye et al 1996).

In order to act confidently, competently and creatively, we need to reflect on our caring intentions; the ends we have in mind and the means we might choose to achieve them. The reflective conversation is the medium through which we do this. The focus on values is a fundamental characteristic of a conversation of this kind. It is one where practitioners interrogate, question and reinterpret the values which guide what they do, in the context within which they find themselves working. Without this characteristic, we suggest that the conversation is not truly reflective but something else, such as a conversation which is more technically focused. Just as some would argue that not all thinking about practice is reflective if there is no questioning of goals and values (Zeichner and Liston 1996), we would assert that a reflective conversation about means and healthcare ends is not reflective if it does not involve a discussion about values. A focus on values gives the supervisee the chance to reveal joys and achievements as values are lived out in practice. Such a focus can also expose the frustrations and contradictions in caring work when values are negated in practice.

Takes an appropriate question-and-answer form

If learning through clinical supervision is about learning through conversation, then it is important for the participants to have a repertoire of questions which enable them to gain some critical distance from their work, to confront aspects of it and to come to know it differently. The questions can be of many kinds (Smyth, 1991), but four fundamental ones are:

- What is my practice like?
- Why is it like this?
- How has it come to be this way?
- What would I like to improve, how and why?

These are challenging questions indeed. Other relevant ones might include:

- How far do I live my caring values out in my work?
- Whose interests are served or denied by my/our practice?
- What organizational and other influences prevent me/us from working in alternative ways?
- Indeed, what alternatives are available?

There are a great many reflective questions (Tomm 1987). The method of conversational analysis described later in this chapter calls different reflective questions 'leads', responses of one kind or another 'reflections', and the various ways in which the participants sustain and develop the conversation 'connections'. Later, we draw upon part of the transcript of one clinical conversation to show how we might answer questions of the following kind:

- How far can the dialogue be described as a conversation?
- How far is it reflective (and therefore values-based, co-operative and creative)?
- What is the evidence to support or refute the above two questions?
- So, what might we learn from using this proposed method of conversational analysis?

The skill of nurturing a reflective conversation is linked to knowing what to ask, when, and in what way. Even more important, in some clinical conversations, is to know when to stop asking questions, to do other things and to enable the silence to be seen as a potentially rich creative space. This is the kind of sensitivity which is not easily 'taught' on such courses as those, for example, which purport to prepare healthcare workers for clinical supervision. Which of our verbal contributions, our listening and thinking contributions, are most helpful when the participants feel they are 'stuck' or in a 'stand-still' situation (Andersen 1991)? It is also about understanding the complexity of human communication and information processing. For example:

> *Human communication is a complex interactive process in which meanings are generated, maintained and/or changed through recursive interaction between human beings. Communication is not to be taken as a simple linear process of transmitting messages from an active sender to a passive receiver; rather, it is a circular, interactive process of co-creation by the participants involved.*
> (Poskiparta et al 1998: 683)

Is located in time and space

The reflective clinical conversation is an artefact of the moment. It is located in time, has antecedents and consequences. In this sense it has a historical dimension. Its co-construction occupies a space, too. What is disclosed is therefore subject to these and other influences. Space has a geographical expression also. So finding a comfortable room or area where a conversation can be developed is fundamental. To add value to reflective conversations, they need to be seen as part of an extended dialogue and, where appropriate, recorded in some mutually acceptable manner, reflected upon and compared over time. In this way, recurring patterns of interest and concern have the chance to emerge. When these are visible and more known we may have more options for action, or acquire insights which might enable us to think differently.

Looks back to what has been

This is probably the most widely accepted view of reflection, and one which describes it as an essentially retrospective activity. But there is a lot more to reflection than this. A commitment to look back is also a commitment to adopt a 'reflective posture'. This idea comes from the work of Freire (1972). He described the hallmarks of this posture as conversationalists examining their experience critically, questioning and interpreting it, and doing this in public and not in isolation from others.

Makes sense of caring work through constructive challenge

Healthcare professionals have to make sense of their work in the situation in which it occurs. They have to make sense of the perceived and actual impact which their caring work has on their clients, their families and their colleagues. In reflective clinical conversations, the important goal is to try to achieve a greater sense of clarity and of certainty that practice was or can be even more clinically effective, professional and ethical. Moving practice forward is stifled if this sense-making quality of the clinical conversation is absent. It is, however, a complex and potentially uncomfortable process and one which is dependent upon a shared commitment from the participants to challenge and confront practice. To move forward implies that we have a greater sense of self and professional identity in relation to practice. In the postmodern (see *Chapter 4*) and de-traditionalizing society described by Glenn (1999: 5–6):

The requirement to construct a personal and professional self, as a continuing process, becomes more acutely necessary than ever before.... To have a self was to be someone of a particular sort; now however, to have a self is to discover who one is through what one does.

Making sense of self through reflections-on-practice needs to be viewed as an active, challenging and creative process of jointly constructed interpretations (Newman and Holzman 1997).

Looks forward to what will or might be

Taylor (1989: 47) suggests that:

In order to have a sense of who we are, we have to have a notion of how we have become and where we are going.

Reflection is not only concerned with looking back, but also with looking forward into the future — with where we are going. Working with experience is the key here. The reflective clinical conversation is centrally about acknowledging the importance of working with experience. In acknowledging this, we should be cautious about simply giving primacy to experience without taking into account the situation in which, and through which, the experience has come about. Clinical experience should not be celebrated uncritically. Simply having experiences to recount in a clinical supervision meeting does not necessarily mean that they are reflected upon in the way in which we are suggesting in this chapter. Meeting for such a conversation should be seen as a context, or facilitating framework, for learning. All such frameworks contain

...taken-for-granted assumptions about what it is legitimate to do, to say and even think.
(Boud and Miller 1996: 18)

Looking into the future is an opportunity to think creatively. Being creative opens up possibilities and avenues for new and improved action.

Has the potential to enlighten and empower

If the clinical conversation is truly reflective, it can also be called co-operative and creative. The creative conversation can be linked to notions of enlightenment and empowerment. This is the subject of another book in this series (Ghaye, Gillespie and Lillyman 2000). In brief, the creative clinical conversation is a process whereby we attempt to add meaning and value to what the participants claim to know and do. This reconstructed and refocused practice can be described as more 'enlightened'. Reflective conversations which are empowering enable us to name, define and construct our own 'realities', to gain a greater sense of control over our professional lives and to develop a more authentic self. However:

> *...it must also be asked whether organizations want an empowered workforce. Indeed to suggest reflection as a process of empowerment suggests that nurses have to assert self against power gradients of more powerful others, whose own interests may be compromised. Nurses may have internalized a sense of the powerless self through working in bureaucratic settings which have taught everyone to be compliant, to be rule governed, and not to ask questions, seek alternatives or deal with competing values.*
> (Johns 1998: 12)

Perhaps the best way to try to improve practice lies not so much in trying to control other people's behaviours, as in helping them to control their own by becoming more aware, through reflection, of what they are doing (Elliott 1987).

Evidence-based practice and the reflective clinical conversation

The reflective clinical conversation touches upon many of those contemporary political and professional initiatives which have been designed to modernize and improve the quality of patient care. It can also be related to what might be regarded as the essence of good caring practice. For example, in *A First Class Service* (NHS Executive 1998), the Government sets out its plans to improve the NHS. The three central elements of these plans are professional self-regulation, clinical governance, and lifelong learning. In very important ways, the reflective clinical conversation makes a real contribution to each element. Reflection — in action and on practice — undertaken in a systematic, sustained, public and constructively critical manner, is indeed a process of individual and collective regulation. It is also to do with self- and group regeneration. This regeneration is linked to the idea that healthcare can, in some extremely significant ways, be 'transformed' through reflective practice (Johns and Freshwater 1998). A commitment to become a reflective practitioner should be a wholehearted and sincere one. We cannot be reflective practitioners on one day and something else on another. Indeed, reflective practitioners appreciate that learning is a continuous interplay between action and reflections on it. They have a commitment, therefore, to the principle of lifelong learning. Reflection should have a consequence. This consequence is that it should try to improve both thinking and clinical practice, and the context in which these take place. Reflective practice is supportive of, and also contributes towards, initiatives for improved clinical effectiveness. If clinical governance is the process by which each part of the NHS quality assures its clinical decisions, then some kind of synergy between this and reflective practice needs to be made.

It goes without saying that practice development must have a firm evidential base. It must be grounded in it and see evidence as its friend, for it is essentially about the process of improvement. So where might we derive such evidence? Reflective practices are an important source, for they are evidence-based. Reflection is not simply a private, solitary, navel-gazing activity where we replay and rehearse, in the comfort of an armchair, some of the things we have recently encountered in our work. Although for some, reflection might have elements of privacy and solitude about it, we should not forget that reflection also has a public and political face. Practice development, or we might call this improvement, is a technical, professional and political activity. It is also essentially judgemental in that we have to make decisions about preferred courses of action, and judgements about what might count as 'a development' or 'an improvement'. In our practice all sorts of improvements can be sensed, explored and tested out. If an agreement can be reached about the need to record our conversations in some appropriate way, the record can become an important source of evidence — the catalyst if you like, for further conversations which have the potential to take practice forward.

The reflective clinical conversation: An example of 'personal-practical' knowledge

One of us (Tony) has been working with a number of clinicians, from a variety of specialities, exploring this idea of a reflective conversation. What follows is a summary of some of his findings drawn from a close textual analysis of 36 transcripts of conversations which were generated through the clinical supervision process (47.25 hours of tape and 427 A4 pages of transcript). The labels 'supervisor' and 'supervisee' are used. The supervision process was organized as a triadic (that is, three-way) relationship, namely supervisor, supervisee and facilitator (Tony).

Tony's role was to analyse the conversation and then re-engage the supervisor and supervisee, some time later, with their original conversation and its analysis. The initial clinical conversation is an example of reflection-on-practice and the re-engagement is an example of meta-reflection, or thinking again about earlier reflections (see *Figure 4.1* on page 56). This re-engagement is a vital part of the learning process. The transcript of the conversation becomes a text to be responded to rather than just read. What can be commented upon in this re-engagement is not only what was said (or thought to be said) but also the rhythm and structure of the conversation as well.

The intentions are to shed further light on the questions:

1. How far can the dialogue be described as a conversation?
2. How far is it reflective (and therefore values-based, co-operative and creative)?
3. What is the evidence to support or refute questions 1 and 2?
4. So, what might we learn from using this proposed method of conversational analysis?

Finding 1: Clinical conversations appear to have three fundamental components:

Leads: what the supervisor said (Sr)

Reflections: what the supervisee said (Se)

Connections: how Sr and Se took turns to sustain the dialogue

Each 'component' has a number of 'sub-parts', and an explanation of each of these follows.

Leads

These are where the supervisor invites the supervisee to present, clarify, understand espoused values and values-in-clinical action.

L(F)• about getting the clinical supervision encounter focused
   • knowing what the Se has 'come with'
   • enabling the Se to make a presentation of the practice incident
   • the beginning, opening Sr move
   • this also refers to a re-focusing strategy by the Sr during the

conversation, re-stating and taking stock of things.

L(P)• invites the Se to present how they felt and now feel about the incident, for example: 'So, how do you feel about things now?'
- invites an affective response
- this is about emotionality.

L(R)• enables the Se to become more aware of other possible views and perspectives on the incident
- the 'lead' enables the Se to 'position' their views/feelings in relation to others
- this is about helping the Se to get things into a more holistic perspective
- this invites the Se to consider alternative frames, for example: 'What about the junior member of staff who was on duty with you? What do you think he/she thought of it?'

L(C)• these are 'leads' which invite the Se to be critical and creative
- they are 'challenging' and invite the Se to question their own and others' practice. They often include the word 'why'
- these often focus in on why things went the way they did; they can challenge routines and the accepted way of doing things
- they focus the Se's attention on a particular point, and can expose contradictions between what is said and what is done
- they invite the Se to make creative connections and leaps. They are used, therefore, to encourage frame movement, for example: 'Why did the patient not get the care that you wanted to give him?'

L(I) • these leads encourage the Se to open up and to own new frames
- these 'leads' are future oriented, 'what-ifs', and aim to encourage the Se to cultivate new/revised/'better' thinking and practice, for example: 'In what ways do you think the situation could be avoided in the future?'

Reflections

This is what the supervisee says. Five types of reflection-on-practice were identified in the data and named thus:

(D) *Descriptive reflections-on-practice*
   The Se describes the practice incident, problem or concern — the start of the 'prime narrative', story or account. It is personally meaningful, concrete and retrospective. This is where the Se's values-in-action become evident. These reflections-on-practice are the 'raw material' with which the Sr and Se where appropriate work.

(P) *Perceptive reflections-on-practice*

The Se expresses personal feelings about the practice incident sensing, in relation to it, discomfort or comfort, disappointment, surprise, joy, anger, frustrations, struggles, fairness, rights. The Se implicitly or explicitly refers to conflicts between espoused values and values-in-action.

(R) *Receptive reflections-on-practice*

Here the Se tries to explain and justify practice. There is an openness and receptivity to alternative views or opinions. A clear intention is conveyed to 'think again' and to reconstruct practice.

(C) *Critical/creative reflections-on-practice*

This type of reflection is where the Se explicitly questions generally accepted clinical routines — the 'taken-for-grantedness' of their work, practices and rituals. In doing so, the status-quo is challenged. Critically reflective comments should not be confused with cynicism and negativity. Principally, they are reflections that place 'local' healthcare practice within a much larger political and professional 'system' — a system that influences, constrains and/or liberates clinical action.

(I) *Interactive reflections-on-practice*

These reflect prospective thinking and interactions between past learning and future action. These future-oriented Se responses involve action language such as, 'I think I will/might... ' and 'I'm going to ... '. The responses are about improvements. They are concerned with moving thinking/practice/clinical context forward. It is where the Se does something with what he/she has learned.

Connections

This is how the supervisor and supervisee sustain and develop the conversation.

s   These are supportive comments — a recognition of the significance of a previous remark, an encouragement to carry on telling. They are comments which encourage movement through the 'prime narrative' in order to decelerate/accelerate the pace of the conversation, for example, 'Yes, go on', 'this is important, tell me more', 'right', 'sure', 'umm', 'uhuh', and so on.

c   These are requests for further clarification of a point being made. They are used if either the Sr or the Se 'loses the plot', for example: 'Can you give me an example of what you mean?', 'What do you mean by that?', 'I don't think I understand what you're trying to say', 'Just go over that again for me, please', 'I'm getting a bit lost here', and so on.

a These are verbal signals of agreement, affirmation, gentle reassurance and approval. They add a degree of harmony to the conversation, for example: 'Right, OK.', 'Yes, I agree with what you are saying', 'Um, that's good that you did that', and so on.

d These are distractions, accidentally built in to the conversation, for example, they could be comments concerned with a necessity to answer the phone or to deal with a person knocking at the door. They also refer to comments used as a deliberate diversion, to take time out, to diffuse the situation, to cool off, for example, 'Can you excuse me a minute while I take this?', 'Let's hold it there for a moment — I'll put the kettle on.'

Finding 2: The components can be used to analyse clinical conversations

What follows is a re-presentation of the conversation used in the *Introduction* to this book, between Sally and Fiona. A practice 'surprise' triggers the reflective process. The dialogue has been analysed, *sentence by sentence*. Each sentence is described by one of the categories above. The whole transcript is therefore *'coded'* and *'scored'*. This gives the participants a quantitative analysis of the nature of their conversation. So, for example, Sally's opening remarks (see below) are coded and scored: L(F)2. This indicates that Sally began the conversation with two *lead-focus* remarks. Fiona then replied with one *s-type (connection)*, nine remarks which are coded as *descriptive reflections-on-practice* and three *perspective type reflections-on-practice*. The codings and scores for the whole conversation can then be placed in a table (see *Table 5.1* on page 83). The table is later used by the facilitator to re-engage Sally and Fiona with their original conversation. Now, the 'headline news' can be discussed and, where appropriate, some detailed discussion can be undertaken about particular parts of the conversation which are regarded as 'critical' in some way. Sometimes the facilitator can ask the participants themselves to 'code and score' segments of the transcript. This not only increases the trustworthiness of the analysis (through respondent validation), but also enables some detailed discussion to take place about 'what reality' and 'whose reality' is being discussed!

Extract from a clinical conversation coded and scored

Sally: Do you want to tell me what happened the other day on the shift, Fiona, because I think you had a bit of a time of it didn't you?   L(F)2

Fiona: Yes ... well. I was on a long day and I was on the late part of the long day with another nurse, and there was a thrombolysis call from casualty. So ... I went down to see the patient who was in Room I with the A and E consultant and one of the casualty doctors. I did a heart trace and the patient, at that time, wasn't coming up to the unit, ... so I went back to the unit. We had one empty bed at the time. We had a very poorly patient in bed 2 who kept having cardiac arrest. He, in fact, had six in all and during one of these cardiac arrests, the patient I had seen down in casualty was wheeled into the middle of the unit during this emergency procedure. We had no prior notification of him coming. He hadn't, in fact, been seen by the SHO who was on and this patient who was new to the unit needed, himself, quite a lot of care. I instructed the nurse to put the patient in a side ward because I was busy with the patient in bed 2 during the cardiac arrest. In fact, I was quite annoyed with the nurse, though it really wasn't her fault for bringing the patient up. After things had calmed down a little she helped me admit the patient, for about five minutes. I did apologise to her and said that I realized it wasn't her fault ... that I would try to sort out who had been responsible for making the decision for the patient being admitted without us knowing.   sl (D)9 (P)3

Sally: So, do you know who authorised the patient to be brought from A and E?   L(D)I

Fiona: It's a bit of a grey area. It was either the consultant who was seeing the patient from A and E, or it was the manager in A and E who was on duty at the time ... or it was the SHO who was on duty... over the phone. There are a few different stories and it's going to be, hopefully, sorted out ... but nobody was claiming responsibility.   (R)3

This whole conversation can now be represented as shown in *Table 5.1*, opposite.

Finding 3: The analysis provides some powerful insights into the nature of the clinical conversation.

Included here are just a few of the insights which can be derived from such a content-analysis of a clinical conversation. The analysis provides the basis for re-engaging the supervisor and supervisee in the meta-reflective process, with the facilitator.

Table 5.1. QUALITIES OF THE CLINICAL CONVERSATION

'Leads (question) and Reflections'

Leads

Score	L (F)	L (D)	L (P)	L (R)	L (C)	L (I)	Total	%
	9	10	5	2	10	3	39	25

→ 25

Reflections

(D)	(P)	(R)	(C)	(I)	Total	%
22	15	25	4	2	68	44

→ 44

'Connective Tissue'

Connections

s	c	a	d	Total	%
24	4	20	0	48	31

Sr:24 — Se:7 — 31

Dialogue	%
Supervisor (Sr):	49
Supervisee (Se):	51

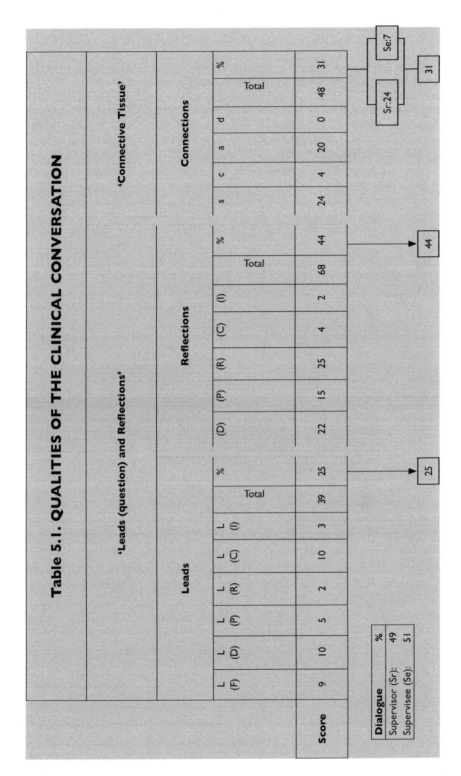

Some observations:

1. There were a total of 155 sentences or speech acts. These comprised the conversation. The supervisee spoke marginally more than the supervisor (51 per cent and 49 per cent, respectively).
2. Twenty five per cent of such speech acts were made up of the supervisor 'leading' the conversation. A further 24 per cent of supervisor speech acts were devoted to strategies to sustain the conversation.
3. Most supervisor 'leads' were L(D), L(C) and L(F) in kind. The supervisee responded by reflecting on practice mainly in receptive and descriptive ways. There was also a relatively high number of speech acts, namely L(P) and (P), which reflected the emotionality and degree of personal feeling in the practice incident presented.
4. Put another way, the supervisor tried to initiate and develop a clinical conversation in two ways. Firstly by inviting the supervisee to frame — L(D) — her clinical concern. Secondly by trying to move the supervisee forward by using a variety of frame-moving strategies — L(C). These two strategies made up 51 per cent of all supervisor 'leads'.
5. The supervisee responded to these leads mainly by drawing upon a receptive type of reflection-on-practice in trying to make sense of the practice incident. Receptive reflection is when the supervisee relates her view of practice and her construction of clinical reality to that of others. The supervisee is receptive and open to alternative perspectives. An additional characteristic of this type of reflection-on-practice is the justifications for practice offered by the supervisee, derived from her own and other people's views of things. So this kind of reflection had some important qualities. It is reflection which generates practical nursing knowledge which is 'positioned'. This means that it is knowledge which is positioned or aligned in relation to some wider and more complex picture. Such a picture would include, for example, the experience of other nurses, in similar and different clinical areas, and knowledge gained from the professional and clinical literature. In receptive reflection-on-practice, the emphasis is on the supervisee reconstructing practice in such a way that she is able to glimpse at and consider new ways of framing the clinical practice incident. However, there is no elaboration and ownership of a new problem frame here and no explicit commitment to any form of future action. This receptive type of reflection comprised 25 individual speech acts, or 37 per cent of everything the supervisee said. It was her most dominant mode of response.
6. The supervisor also devoted a considerable amount of her time to L(F) and L(C). These are remarks which invite the supervisee to focus or refocus, and to make 'creative connections'. In other words, it is

Sally's way of trying to move Fiona's thinking forward. She can justify this because of Fiona's dominant way of reflecting-on-practice (see 5 above). The dominance of these particular 'leads' is an important part of this clinical conversation. Such dominance has the power to make the conversation both reflective (values-focused) and creative. Without skilful and confident supervisors who can reflect-in-action (as the conversation unfolds in front of them), any opportunities for clinical conversations to be reflective and creative are lost.

Some meta-reflections

This analysis serves to remind us of Principle 8, introduced earlier, that *the reflective conversation is at the heart of the process of reflecting-on-practice*. It is the medium and vehicle which enables the participants to move thinking, practice and perhaps the clinical context in which the two are embedded, forward in some way. This conversation is much more than coffee and a chat. It is an enabling process; reflective and creative in kind. For this type of conversation to come about, much more attention needs to be given to the quality of the interaction between the participants, how it can be initiated, nourished and learned from.

This system of conversational analysis enables the participants clearly to identify what was said, as opposed to what they thought was said. The reality question again! The system can foster further reflection, and therefore discussion, about the usefulness of the conversation for practice. This can also be related to participant expectations (what they thought they would/should/ might get out of the conversation), roles and responsibilities (who does what and why) and impact on care (what is taken away from the conversation, what action is planned and the creative ways forward envisaged). The system is also re-constructive in the sense that the analysis allows us to de-construct the 'prime narrative', to look again at what was said, to engage in the process of meta-reflection and then finally put the narrative back together again. Arguably, this reconstruction process is creative. The re-constructed narrative also connects closely to the 'reflective promise' that the process enables the participants to become more enlightened and also, perhaps, more empowered and emancipated. If, as in this case, the supervisee feels that she is getting little from the conversation, that it is not helping her to move forward, then the analysis will help to point to a possible explanation for this.

The triadic conversation itself addresses the issue of 'insider knowledge' and the role of the 'external perspective' in clinical practice. It raises the questions, 'Who actually needs to know what in a clinical conversation?'

and 'Who does what? In the approach proposed, the role of the third party is crucial as analyst and facilitator. The third party analyses the transcript and summarizes its main features. Supervisor and supervisee are then invited to reflect on this analysis. A three-way conversation then takes place, based on evidence. This is the essential and much neglected process of meta-reflection. Reflecting on earlier reflections anchors learning and re-frames clinical experience. It is not necessary for the third party to be from the same clinical area, specialism, directorate or trust.

Reflective clinical conversations are about healthcare values (see *Chapter 6*) and creative action. This mode of analysis, which is evidence based, is therefore very much a part of enhancing clinical effectiveness. It turns conversation into a research process (Feldman, 1999) and its participants into healthcare practitioner/researchers. Delivering a clinically effective service must involve a consideration of any research relevant to that service. Participants in reflective clinical conversations will require skills in generating practical healthcare knowledge of the kind suggested here; skills in making sense of that knowledge; strategies to use what they claim to know; and competence, confidence and sensitivities to evaluate the effects of this 'better knowledge' on the delivery of a clinically effective service.

Reflective clinical conversations are essentially an exercise in the construction of realities — through the conversational process we build meanings and construct identities for ourselves within a cultural, historical, clinical and political context. We co-construct and re-construct realities. Personal realities differ. We all see things differently. In and through reflective conversations we can explore these different realities. By so doing, practice becomes a process of coming to know. It is a way of revealing a reality to ourselves and giving ourselves the opportunity to transform that reality. It is, therefore, not only potentially creative but is also a liberating process.

The final point we wish to make brings us full circle to the whole business of valuing our own personal-practical healthcare knowledge and not just the knowledge of others. One of the most divisive, inhibiting, oppressive and pervasive beliefs in much of healthcare is that the only knowledge worth having and knowing is that which is 'scientific' and propositional in kind. This is knowledge which is derived from randomized control trials, from large samples, which uses a hypothetico-deductive approach. It is knowledge which claims to be generalizable and universally 'true'. It also carries with it the spurious label of being 'objective' knowledge and of having a sense of 'certainty'. Whilst not denying the value of knowledge of this kind for certain purposes, we do believe that a more empowered, accountable and satisfied workforce requires a significant reversal in our usual answer to the question, 'So what knowledge is worth knowing?' Just as reality is ambiguous and uncertain, so too is knowledge. Really worthwhile knowledge can be generated in many ways. Reflective clinical conversations are those in which healthcare professionals value and celebrate co-constructed, 'personal-practical' knowledge from the descriptions, explanations and justifications they give of their own local practice. Arguably, this is the essence of a lifelong learning process.

References

Andersen T, ed. (1991) *The Reflecting Team: Dialogues and Dialogues about Dialogues.* W. Norton and Company, New York

Boud D, Miller N (1996) *Working with Experience: Animating Learning.* Routledge,London

Cochran-Smith M, Lytle S (1993) *Inside/outside: Teacher research and knowledge.* Teacher's College Press, New York

Elliott J (1987) Educational theory, practical philosophy and action research. *Br J Educ Studies* **35:** 149–69

Feldman A (1996) Enhancing the practice ofphysics teachers: mechanisms for the generation of sharing knowledge and understanding in collaborative action research. *J Res Science Teaching* **33:** 513–40

Feldman A (1999) The Role of Conversation in Collaborative Action Research. *Educ Action Res* **J7**(1): 125–44

Freire P (1972) *Pedagogy of the Oppressed.* Penguin, Harmondsworth

Ghaye T, Cuthbert S, Danai K, et al (1996) *Professional Values: Being a Professional, Learning through Critical Reflective Practice: Self-Supported Learning Experiences for Healthcare Professionals.* Pentaxion Press, Newcastle upon Tyne

Ghaye T, Gillespie, D, Lillyman S, eds (2000) *Empowerment Through Reflection: The narratives of healthcare professionals.* Mark Allen Publishing, Salisbury

Ghaye T, Lillyman S, eds (2007) *Effective Clinical Supervision: The role of reflection.* 2nd edition. Mark Allen Publishing, Salisbury

Glenn S (1999) Health Care Education for dialogue and dialogic relationships. *Nurs Ethics* **6**(1): 3–11

Hollingsworth S (1994) *Teacher research and urban literacy education: lessons and conversations in a feminist key.* Teachers College Press, New York

Johns C (1998) Opening the Doors of Perception. In: JoOOs C, Freshwater D eds. *Transforming Nursing through Reflective Practice.* Blackwell Science, Oxford

Johns C, Freshwater D, eds (1998) *Transforming Nursing through Reflective Practice.* Blackwell Science, Oxford

Newman F, Holzman L (1997) *The End of Knowing: A new developmental way of knowing.*

Routledge, London

NHS Executive (1998) *A First Class Service: Quality in the New NHS*. NHS Executive, Leeds

Polanyi M (1958) *Personal Knowledge*. Oxford University Press, Oxford

Poskiparta M, Kettunen T, Liimatainen L (1998) Reflective Questions in Health Counselling. *Qualitative Health Res* **8**(5): 682–93

Schön D (1987) *Educating the Reflective Practitioner*. Jossey Bass, London

Schön D (1983) *The Reflective Practitioner: How professionals think in action*. Basic Books, New York

Senge P (1992) *The Fifth Discipline: The Art and Practice of the Learning Organisation*. Century Business, London

Smyth J (1991) *Teachers as Collaborative Learners*. Open University Press, Milton Keynes

Taylor C (1989) *Sources of the Self*. Cambridge University Press, Cambridge

Tomm K (1987) Interventive Interviewing: Part 11 Reflective questioning as a means to enable self-healing. *Family Process* **26:** 167–83

Zeichner K, Liston D (1996) *Reflective Teaching: An Introduction*. Lawrence Earlbaum Associates, New Jersey

CHAPTER 6

Reflections on values: Being a professional

'So, what kind of healthcare professional am I?' This is a challenging question. It is also one we do not often get asked. To answer it, we have to be honest with ourselves. We have to know ourselves. This, at least, involves reflecting on what we do and how and why we do it. Describing our clinical, professional and managerial work is a good starting point. After this we need to try to explain and then justify our caring work. We need to do this for ourselves and to others when called upon to do so. Our values play a key role in this process.

Throughout our professional lives we think and behave in certain ways and believe in certain things, such as how far our work can be described as 'caring', 'professional', 'educational', and so on. We reflect upon what we feel we can offer to our patients, the organization and our profession. We think about what our strengths and capabilities are. What we do, think and feel about our healthcare work constitutes our sense of professional identity. We reveal and communicate this identity when we address and answer the question, 'So what kind of healthcare professional am I?'

It is our values which give our work its shape, direction and purpose. Our values make us the kind of person we are. They provide us with reasons for doing what we do, in the way that we do it. They are a fundamental part of our professional identity and sense of self. If we look at our own clinical work, and when we observe the work of others, we should expect to see an effort being made to put into practice those things we value. After all, these things are called values because we 'value' them, 'care' for them and passionately believe in them. Our personal-professional values belong to us. We may not always be able to put these values into practice to our full satisfaction, but we should, however, make an effort to try to do so.

We are therefore highlighting a link between identity, values and clinical actions. Two experienced nurses, undertaking a BA (Ed) Honours Degree in Reflective Practice at the University of Worcester, expressed this connection in the form of a 'reflective rap'. We thank Fay and Shirley for allowing us to draw upon their work.

Our Reflective Rap

My name is Fay
My name is Shirley
We look alike
With hair that's curly

Being a professional
Is what we do
With Tony saying
What kind are you?

We both have values
Honest and sound
In the Coronary Care Unit
Where we are found

We talk and reflect
On our clinical skills
Whilst tending to patients
And dishing out pills

A quality service
We aim to provide
Reflective practice being
A trusted guide

So with positive feelings
True values win through
Reflecting on practice
Is the thing to do

Although a light-hearted form of representation, Fay and Shirley's rap contains some important messages. In clarifying our allegiance to a set of values, we might find that we do not become attached to a particular set of values which never changes. It is important to be open to the possibility that our values may change over time, with experience and insight, and as the clinical contexts in which we work change. As we search for greater self-understanding, more robust rationales for what we do and a greater consistency in trying to live out our values in our caring work, the sense that all our values are static and fixed entities may be far from our lived reality. Our values can and do change. This is quite natural. We suggest that at the point of entry to, for example, the nursing profession, newly qualified individuals have a set of personally-owned professional values. Hopefully nurses are able to articulate and defend these and know how to respond in a clinical environment, or culture, when encountering others who hold conflicting or alternative values equally as strongly as themselves.

We cannot base our work together for the common good, on reticence, embarrassment and incoherent mumbling, yet this is the state into which the discussion of morals and values has descended in many parts of Western society today.
(Carey 1997: 3)

In order to be called a professional and to be convincing, safe, and accountable for what we do, it is not simply appropriate for us to say that we think we are doing a good job. Proclaiming is not enough in today's healthcare context. Good, safe and accountable practice needs to be demonstrated. The art and science of caring is one that needs constant renewal and reworking. In order that it does not disintegrate, and with it our sense of professional identity and self-worth, it is imperative that the process of regeneration coheres around a set of professional values which we own and can justify. This justification depends upon the process of constantly reflecting on these values and communicating them clearly and persuasively to others when necessary.

Given these introductory statements about values it is, at this point, appropriate to anchor them with the ninth principle of reflective practice, which is:

> **Principle 9: Reflection emphasizes the links between values and actions**

Nixon (1995) helpfully states that the links between values and actions need constant qualification and refinement. This is especially so in a fast-changing healthcare system. Our clinical actions are, in fact, our 'values-in-use'. The things we say about our practice are our espoused values (see *Chapter 4*); the things we actually do are our values-in-use. The two might not always match up! Arguably, we can only really call ourselves professionals if the values which we espouse are professed in and through our practice. So, we need to work out our values. We suggest that this is done through meaningful dialogues in reflective clinical teams. In other words, not in isolation and abstraction but through collaboration and negotiation with colleagues in the midst of the complexities of clinical life.

So, what do you do?

Creating descriptions of practice is an important way to begin to understand Principle 9. Doing this fulfils two important purposes. Firstly, it creates an account which we can go on to question and tease apart by reflecting on it. Reflection-on-practice has the power to change something which we might not fully understand or have control and influence over, into something with more personal clarity, coherence and meaning. Secondly, the descriptions provide us with the evidence of the values which form the rationale for our caring-healing work. An account imbued with values is presented below. We thank Esther for placing this in the public domain. Esther called her account, 'Advocacy'.

Advocacy

Mrs A was transferred to our ward accompanied by her daughter and son-in-law. Mrs A was 76 and prior to her admission she had been living in a rest home was fully ambulant and independent with her activities of daily living. Dementia had impeded her cognition. She was hospitalized to undergo a cholecystectomy and unfortunately a pneumothorax presented as a post-operative complication. Following this, and whilst still in hospital, she sustained a brain stem cerebrovascular accident (usually called a stroke). Whilst I checked the intravenous fluids, catheter and positioning of Mrs A, her daughter chatted to me about her mother. This all assisted my information gathering as part of my initial assessment. Mrs A's cholecystectomy and chest drain wounds seemed to be healing well. Her skin was intact and regular mouth care had kept her oral mucosa moist.

Mrs A gradually improved and soon we had her sitting in a chair for two hours each morning. Her swallow reflex had also improved and she was commenced on thickened fluids and a pureed diet. Intravenous fluids were discontinued. She could communicate with a word here and there but cognition seemed to be greatly impaired.

One morning all was not well. Mrs A had had a shower, as usual, but her balance seemed to have deteriorated and she seemed very sleepy. We put her back to bed and had her reassessed by the medical staff. She had had an extension of her cerebrovascular accident. The nil-by-mouth sign went back up, subcutaneous fluids commenced and two-hourly comfort care began.

Mrs A's daughter helped me turn her mother and comb her hair. I would cleanse her mouth. Often she required suctioning. I've always been a bit wary of suctioning, but together, her daughter supporting her flaccid neck, and me using the equipment, we would free the gurgling secretions. I gained great satisfaction in hearing quiet breath sounds.

On one occasion I was off for two days. On my return to work I was asked by the doctors to insert a tube for feeding. Two previous attempts had apparently been unsuccessful. Mrs A had to be restrained as she resisted so much and it seemed I could only get it down so far and no further. Mrs A cried out, 'No more, no more'. I did not believe she was consenting to the procedure. The doctors were doing their round and arrived in the room. I explained to them what had happened and that it seemed clear that Mrs A did not want the tube and that it was not going in easily anyway. 'Would you like me to try?' said the doctor. 'Well... not really,' I replied. 'You see, I'm convinced Mrs A doesn't want the tube.' (This felt scary...) Consequently the tube stayed out. Being an advocate felt good.

Our next hurdle was the medical staff's wish to insert a gastrostomy tube. Here's our ethical dilemma. Feed or not to feed. Prolong life or allow nature to take its course. I saw before me the agony of a daughter, dedicated to her mother's welfare, tossed to and fro as she prepared herself for a family meeting in which her mother's future (or no future) would be decided. As a nurse, I personally felt extremely unhappy about further medical intervention. What's wrong with a peaceful death?

Mrs A's daughter had very strong religious beliefs and she grappled with, on one hand, the guilt of allowing her mother to die whilst on the other, knowing the reality that her Mum had so little left to live for. She had no use of her body, she had dementia and the dying process had apparently already begun. How it struck me again that a nurse cares for the whole family.

Mrs A's daughter decided to 'trust in God' for the outcome. The family meeting was to be Monday. Mrs A died peacefully Sunday night, her family surrounding her.

I went to the funeral. Why? For myself mainly. I had been a part of that family for five weeks, experienced their joys and pains, their agonising decision-making and the unity of family members around a hospital bed. It touched them deeply that I came. That felt rewarding. So... being a nurse is not just giving, it's making connections with people and receiving from them the strength to go on in a profession of caring.

There is much to reflect upon here as Esther constantly reveals links between her values and her clinical practice. Indeed, there are many values 'tangled-up' in this account. Some important links are being made with regard to a number of aspects of practice such as risk assessment, decision-making, the ethics of care, dying and death, pain, managing stress and anxiety, and conducting very difficult conversations. Being the patient's advocate is a central value, held and lived out by Esther. She said it 'felt good' but it was also 'scary'. This says much about advocacy in healthcare. There are pros and cons depending upon what type of advocacy we have in mind.

> *Advocacy is about power. It means influencing those who have power on behalf of those who do not ... . In other words, advocacy is required when people feel vulnerable and powerless.*
> (Teasdale 1998: 1)

There are other values we can disentangle from Esther's account. For example, there are values in relation to self-determination, rights, holistic care and patient autonomy. These values give Esther a clear sense of self and professional identity, and do much to counter the stereotypes of nursing, prevalent for example in the media and public consciousness, which are negative, confusing and inaccurate. These stereotypes are not easily erased. Articulating the values which underpin practice is a way of challenging some of the image and identity problems which still remain. What is also clear in Esther's account is a view of nursing which is not solely about body-physical acts, but which embraces mind-body-spirit. As she lives out her values in her practice, there is a sense of 'being' as well as of 'knowing' and 'doing'. Watson (1999: 10) puts it beautifully:

> *It calls forth from the practitioner an authentic presencing of being in the caring moment, carrying an intentional caring-healing consciousness.*

and later (p.15):

> *Caring and healing are about relation, not separation, about meaning, being and finding sacredness in the act of caring itself. This in turn, becomes what Whitehead (1953) called the 'eternal now' — a timeless, transcendent moment for humankind.*

The articulation of our values and their justification forms a 'text' which can be used to reveal the ways these texts differ from the 'medical text'. These texts (which we describe and present in Ghaye and Lillyman 2000, as 'caring moments') may only be 'marginal texts' at present, but they do offer the possibility of:

> *...new vistas of being in the world, perceiving new patterns and possibilities for caring and healing of self, other and life itself.*
> (Watson 1999: 18)

On the nature of values

'Values' is a contentious and slippery word in healthcare. For us, a value is something which is socially constructed, consciously and critically reflected upon, and evidenced in our actions with our patients/clients and colleagues. In this sense, our view of values shares many of the attributes of what Carr (1992) calls 'principled preferences'. He argues that 'principled preferences' are of 'quite considerable importance' and that:

> *... unlike other sorts of preferences which are based merely on personal taste or natural disposition, values are standardly a consequence of something approaching intelligent deliberation and are thus, in principle, susceptible to rational appraisal and re-appraisal.*
> (Carr 1992: 244)

Healthcare professionals are making choices every minute of their working hours. Each of these choices implies an underlying value, a 'because' or an 'ought'. This makes healthcare professionals valuing beings, and healthcare a value-laden enterprise.

Values are everywhere — in the culture of *Shaping the Future of Care Together* (DoH, 2009), in the plans for a National Family-Parenting Institute, in the Sure Start initiative and in the development of Health Action Zones, in clinical governance, in the work of Primary Care Groups, Primary Care Investment Plans and Health Improvement Programmes. But they do not float around in some kind of void. Neither do they:

> *...grow on trees or fall like manna from heaven. They do not just look after themselves. On the contrary, they are always vulnerable to the darker side of human nature such as selfishness, greed, self-deception, vanity, lust and cowardice.*
> (Carey 1997: 2)

Values are located historically. They come from somewhere. They are also located socially, culturally and politically. They exist in what we say or choose not to say. In what we do or do not do. Values can be heard in meetings of educational consortia, research and development groups and at Trust Board meetings, for example. They can be read about in such official documents as mission statements and strategic plans, in *The National Health Improvement Plan* (DoH, 2004), and in *Building the National Care Services* (2010). Values are reflected in the artefacts which may or may not adorn the clinical areas in which we work. They are reflected in the way we speak to each other, for example at those times when we hear the use of the word 'we' rather than 'I'. This conveys values to do with teamwork, collegiality, and the way staff support each other. Values are reflected in our patterns of behaviour, especially in the form of rites, rituals, ceremonies and celebrations.

These behaviours can serve to reinforce directorate, ward, department, unit and service values, and to bond people together. Values can give clinical teams a sense of belonging, of shared commitment and understanding which is central to a collective sense of moral purpose and accountability. But they can also serve to disunite them and highlight differences between individuals and groups. The expectations of individuals and groups are sometimes in conflict. The corridors, coffee corners, committee rooms and other arenas of healthcare work, can become the battleground where different groups, with different values, vie for influence and domination.

Differences in values, then, can lead to conflict. But this does not necessarily have to be destructive. Differences can be resolved if there is a will, a determination, an openness and receptiveness to other points of view and, perhaps, to compromise. But:

> ...the way in which we see our own values and the kind of significance they have for us, will affect our attitude towards compromise.
> (Haydon 1997: 53)

It is most important to appreciate that we can feel threatened and vulnerable when our values clash with those of others. Values can give us a shared language yet can also be used to illustrate how difficult it is sometimes to be heard and understood by others, especially when struggling to work in a multi-disciplinary and inter-agency way. We believe that it is important to reflect on our individual and collective values in the light of recent government reforms, growing cultural diversity, the voice of the consumer of health services, recruitment and retention issues, morale, increasing uncertainty about and media attention to what a national health service for the 21st century in the UK needs to, might or should be. If values in society are controversial and contentious, then it is not surprising that values in healthcare are slippery and contestable also. Taking the spirit of Lather (1991), a challenge for us all at the start of a new millennium, is how far we can learn from our experiences and become what we are destined to become. Do the range of caring professions have to remain part of the hegemony of a Western model of medicine and science? Perhaps we need a new lens for seeing and therefore for knowing and doing. Reflection is one such lens which allows for such a transformation.

How far do values come from within us?

Here are two values. One is more elaborate then the other. Jane is an experienced district nurse. One of her values is:

I believe that everyone should be motivated to look at their own professional development because it allows people to realize the skills and attributes they already have and can highlight areas for further development.
(Ghaye et al 1996: 21)

Julia is an experienced nurse caring for those with mental health problems. One of her values is:

I believe that each patient that I am responsible for is worthy of my constant care and attention because each one has mental health problems unique to them and needs professional attention... and yet... time and resources prevent this, resulting in nurses being involved in intensive care or crisis management with people with less 'risky/acute' problems taking the back seat.
(Ghaye et al 1996: 30)

There are a number of things to notice here. The articulation of these values have a particular structure. They begin with, 'I believe that... (or 'I believe in...'). Then we come across the word, 'because...'. This word begins the justification for holding the value. Simply articulating a value is not enough. Values in themselves do not, by right, occupy some moral high ground. We have to be able to justify holding our particular set of values. The inclusion of the phrase, 'and yet...' in Julia's value, signals to us that we often have some difficulty in living out the values we hold.

It might be useful to try to set down in writing the values you hold in this way. It might be quite illuminating if you did this with a colleague or within your clinical team. It might also be useful to limit yourself to those values which you would regard as 'core' values. These are the ones which you have held for some time. They have stayed with you. You have tried to look after them and live them out in your work. They are the values you certainly would not wish to compromise. They speak loudly about your sense of self-worth and professional identity. These are the ones which also help us to develop a sense of 'agency'. This means that they help us to do things, to initiate improved ways of working and to provide a rationale for these actions. One consequence of committing our values to paper is that we are more able to hold ourselves and each other accountable for our actions. This is the link with Principle 4 — *reflective practice is about learning how to account positively for ourselves.*

When you have set out your core values, we suggest that you 'test' your commitment to them by asking yourself the following questions.

- How far did I choose my core values freely?
- How far were my core values chosen from a set of alternative values?
- How far am I able to articulate the consequences of holding these values for myself, my patients and my organization?
- How far are these values which I care passionately about?
- How far are these values publicly affirmed and supported by those I work with and for?
- How far do I try to live these values out in my everyday work?
- How far do I 'hang in there' and not let these values go, or compromise them when faced with difficulties in living them out?

Reflection-on-practice reveals to us the links between values and action. Without such reflections we may never really know what they are. More to the point, we may never come up with a convincing answer to the question, 'So what kind of professional am I?'

Values from 'elsewhere'

Value statements are everywhere. Because none of us works in isolation (this is different from working alone), but rather within a 'system', it is prudent to be aware of the values which impact upon us from 'elsewhere'. By this, we mean from outside of our organization. Such values serve both to liberate and to constrain us. Apart from value statements in documents from those 'authorities' we mentioned in *Chapter 3*, a major source of such values comes in the form of Government pronouncements of one colour or another. When New Labour talks about a 'modern and dependable NHS' (DoH, 1997a), it is stating a value position. The White Paper is full of values. For example, in the first paragraph it states that (paragraph 1.1):

The Government is committed to giving the people of this country the best system of healthcare in the world.

In paragraph 1.5 we find:

The Government has committed itself anew to the historic principle of the NHS; that if you are ill or injured there will be a national health service there to help; and access to it will be based on need and need alone — not on your ability to pay, or on who your GP happens to be or on where you live.

When Government says, 'The needs of patients will be central to the new system' (paragraph 1.4), it is espousing a clear value. Later in the White

Paper we find the Government hinting at the difficulty we were describing earlier, namely a realization that espousing values is one thing, values-in-action is something quite different. For example (paragraphs 1.15–1 7):

> *... Some say that this vision is not just ambitious, but unachievable... They believe that the NHS is being overwhelmed by three big pressures: growing public expectations, medical advances and demographic changes... Those who argue that the NHS cannot accommodate these pressures say that it will need huge increases in taxation, a move to a charge-based service, or radical restrictions in patient care.*

Not surprisingly, the Government refutes this analysis.

How far are healthcare values contested?

For many in healthcare a particularly pervasive value is, 'that which can be measured and quantified is deemed to be important and worthwhile to know'. This was given added spice when Cochrane (1971) argued persuasively that to achieve optimum results from the NHS, much more needed to be known about the costs and benefits of clinical activities. Although there is an increasing recognition of the dangers of pursuing those things which are statistically significant but humanly insignificant, empirical quantifiable data still occupy the high ground in the debate about clinical effectiveness and evidence-based healthcare (CSAG 1998).

This example usefully serves to raise a number of fundamental problems which we need to reflect upon and resolve locally. These problems make values contestable. The first is the problem of 'What values do we hold?' The second is, 'Which values have (or appear to have) more legitimacy and authority?' By this, we mean 'Which values are more appropriate in what contexts?' The first problem, then, is about what the values actually are. The second is a normative problem of what they should or might be. These are different issues. Thirdly, there is the problem of knowing how to reconcile the differences between values. In the context of clinical teams and their relationship with the organization, it is the issue of knowing what to do when colleagues either do not appreciate, or wish to subscribe to, a particular value or values. Clearly, it is very important for us to reflect upon value disagreements. What happens if we value self-determination, autonomy and independence when all those around us value collegiality, collaboration and teamwork? Finally, there is the problem of how we might most competently and confidently live out our individual and collective values in our caring work. Values are really only meaningful in the context of the clinical, social and political space from which they emerge. Old lists of values should not hinder the creation of new ones which form the basis of improved action. They should not be a ball and chain around our feet.

Some believe that the search for common values may well be something of an aspiration rather than a reality in a culturally pluralistic world. Alternatively, others argue that common values need to be sought out and agreed and that these shared values need not be bland, obvious and uninteresting. The common values which a clinical team, for example, might set out, need to be debated and defended with passion as well as with reason, just like our own personal-professional values lived out with our own patients, their families and with our colleagues.

Additionally, some dominant groups in healthcare have the power to impose meanings and values on others. This can be a great source of frustration for individuals. It can lead to conflict which erodes confidence, destroys teams and leads to a disenchanted workforce. Alternatively, it can lead to the reproduction of values which prop up and legitimise the dominant group (Gramsci 1971, Bourdieu 1994). The last point we wish to make here is that certain values have more transformative potential than others. For example, care and compassion may be important values which give our work its shape, form and purpose. Living these values out in relation to individual patients may be a considerable achievement, but they may not be sufficient to change the culture of the organization which undermines such values by promoting cost-effectiveness and efficiency by being input-output oriented, ever-conscious of league tables, performance indicators and benchmarks!

What is the link between values and action?

Whitehead (1985, 1989, 1993, 1996) has made an extremely significant contribution to the debate about the link between values and action. We have already discussed the essence of his contribution to knowledge creation in *Chapter 3* (Turning personal-practical knowledge into 'living theory'). Whitehead also encourages us to make a response to the following fundamental question: 'How do I improve my practice here?' Notice the question's constituents: 'How' is anticipatory in nature and forward looking. It also suggests a process of enquiry to be entered into. The 'I' is central and places us in the middle of our own action. 'I' can be replaced by 'we' in appropriate circumstances, especially if we are trying to improve the practice of clinical teams. The 'I' in Whitehead's question is a 'living I'. In our view it arises, in part, from the way we act within and upon the world. It suggests a level of awareness of the 'me' or our multiple selves within the process of improvement. This awareness is nourished by our ability to be reflective.

The 'living I' lives in the worlds of the actual, the possible and the desirable. The word 'improve' is an intentional term. It is the main intention of entering into the process of action-reflection-action. It is what we hope to achieve (see *Chapter 9*). 'Practice' is what we do, or think we do! It is the 'what' in the improvement process. Finally, including the word 'here' reminds us that our practice, and our commitment to try to improve aspects of it, needs to be understood in a context (see *Chapter 10*).

Earlier we suggested that it is not always possible to live out our values fully in our practice. Things can get in the way. Whitehead (1992) presents the explanatory and liberating notion of the 'I' existing as a 'living contradiction'. He puts it this way (p.6):

> ...*think about how you have tried to overcome problems in your professional practice. I think such a reflection will reveal that you have experienced a tension in holding certain values and experiencing their negation at the same time in your practice.*

These tensions are well illustrated in the following statements, both of which are made by experienced healthcare professionals:

> *I believe parents should be allowed to stay with their children in our department at all times, but because some consultants do not allow this, I am always asking parents to go, so I am always in conflict. Parents have rights.*
> (Diane)

> *I believe that I should give total patient care, wholeheartedly and uninterrupted, not only attending to physical needs but emotional needs also. But the state of the NHS and the lack of resources in my clinical area means that I am not allowed to do this. I feel frustrated.*
> (Melody)

Put simply, we often say we value something, for example having regular, open meetings with staff on the ward to encourage shared decision-making, and then we do the opposite. We make decisions and do not consult others. Here we exist as a living contradiction. When, for example, I say that I value quality bedside time with all my patients, and then find that I concentrate only on those who need or attract my attention, I am denying my values in my practice. We can view contradictions as growth points, as tensions and struggles which need to be reflected upon. They can form the basis for systematic reflections-on-practice (see *Chapter 8*). Sometimes we can feel a sense of powerlessness when experiencing contradictions.

Sometimes, through reflection of one kind or another (see *Chapter 5*) we can develop new appreciations about what is, or is not possible. There may be times when we just have to say, 'Well, that's how it is here right now and there isn't a great deal that I can do about things for the time being!'

It is too simplistic to think that practice moves smoothly and without problems from values being negated in practice to a position where we do live them out. Moving forward might involve some kind of creative synthesis of previous contradictions. Accountable clinical action is about accepting responsibility for making sincere, transparent, systematic and convincing efforts to try to live out our values, as fully as possible, in our professional practice. The ways in which we might know how far we actually do this, and the role of reflection-on-practice in the process, are the subjects of the *Chapter 8*.

References

Bourdieu P (1994) *Reproduction in Education, Society and Culture*. Sage Publications, London

Carey G (1997) Moral values -the challenge and the opportunity. unpublished paper presented at the Values and the Curriculum Conference, Institute of Education, University of London

Carr W, (1992) Practical enquiry, values and the problem of educational theory. *Oxford Review of Education* **18** (3): 241-51

Cochrane A (1971) *Effectiveness and Efficiency*. The Nuffield Provincial Hospitals Trust, London

DoH (2004) The NHS improvement plan: Putting People at the heart of public services. DoH: London

DoH (2009) Shaping the Future of care Together. DoH London

DoH (2010) Building the national care service. DoH London.

Ghaye T et al (1996) *Professional Values: Being a Professional, Learning through Critical Reflective Practice: Self-supported Learning Experiences for Healthcare Professionals*. Pentaxion Press, Newcastle-upon-Tyne

Ghaye T, Lillyman S, eds (2000) *Caring Moments: The discourse of reflective practice*. Mark Allen Publishing, Salisbury

Gramsci A (1971) Selections from *Prison Notebooks*. New Left Books, New York

Haydon, G (1997) *Teaching about Values: A new approach*. Cassell, London

Lather P (1991) *Getting Smart: feminist research and pedagogy within the post-modern*. Routledge, New York

Nixon J (1995) *Teaching as a profession of values.* in Smyth J, ed. Critical Discourses on Teacher Development. Cassell, London Teasdale K (1998) Advocacy in Health Care. Blackwell Science, Oxford Watson J (1999) Post-modern Nursing and Beyond. Churchill Livingstone, London

Whitehead A (1953) *Science and the Modern World.* Cambridge University Press, Cambridge

Whitehead J (1985) *The analysis of an individual's educational development.* in Shipman M, ed. Educational Research: Principles, Policies and Practice. The Falmer Press, London

Whitehead J (1989) *Creating a living educational theory from questions of the kind, 'How do I improve my practice?'* Cambridge J Education 19 (1): 41-52

Whitehead J (1992) *An account of an individual's educational development.* Action Research Group, School of Education, University of Bath, UK

Whitehead J (1993) *The Growth of Educational Knowledge: Creating your own living educational theories.* Hyde Publications, Bournemouth

Whitehead J (1996) *Living my values more fully in my practice.* in Lomax P, Selley N, eds Supporting critical communities through an educational action research network. Kingston Hill Action Research Group, Kingston University, UK

CHAPTER 7

The value of reflection for continuing professional development

Introduction

Continuing professional development (CPD) is no longer a luxury that professionals can afford to ignore. With constantly changing and improving clinical practice in the healthcare arena, as Darzi states, 'to stand still is to fall back' (DoH 2009: 4/5). Therefore to develop practice and provide quality care all healthcare practitioners are required to engage in CPD. Although many professional bodies identify statutory standards for CPD this development must become personal if we are to maintain a quality service.

This chapter reviews some of the professional bodies and government standards for CPD. We also look at how practitioners can use reflection to develop as professionals, and maintain standards of care whilst meeting Government, professional and organizational requirements.

What is CPD?

Continuing professional development is the way health professionals continue to learn and develop throughout their careers so they keep their skills and knowledge up to date to work safely and effectively.
(Health Professional Council 2008: 1)

This 'learning and development' can be gained through formal ongoing education, training, attendance at conferences, reading, research, personal reflections on practice, etc. Some professional bodies note a timeframe for the CPD, i.e. the Royal College of Surgeons of England require 250 hours over two years. However the nature and type of activity to maintain professional competence seems to be determined by the individual and is often not as an integral part of professional activity within the context of work (Munro 2008) resulting in a gap between what we know and what we practise.

Meeting professional bodies' requirements

Continuing professional development is essential to all healthcare staff whatever their professional background or place of work. For those working within the NHS, with the exception of dentists and doctors and some board level and other senior managers who have separate arrangements for their development review, the *Knowledge and Skills Framework* (KSF) (DoH 2004), sets out standards for all employees. This framework focuses on the application of knowledge and skills, however it is not specific in the knowledge required and the skills people need to develop.

Professionals working outside of the NHS are still governed by their respective professional bodies. Many of these professional bodies set minimal CPD requirement as essential in order for the practitioner to re-register for annual or five yearly registrations. Professionals working within the NHS have to meet both the KSF requirements and those set down by their professional bodies.

Health Professional Council

The Health Professional Council (HPC) set out their standards and include the following professional practitioners; arts therapist, biomedical scientists, chiropodists/podiatrists, dieticians, occupational therapists, operating department practitioners, orthoptists, physiotherapists, psychologists, prosthetics/orthotists, radiographers and speech and language therapists.

The HPC (2005) states in its standards that professionals must maintain a continuous and accurate record of their CPD activities; demonstrate those activities are a mixture of learning activities relevant to their future and current practice; seek to ensure that their CPD has contributed to their practice and benefits the service user; and can produce a written profile containing evidence of their CPD on request. They do however allow for flexibility and diverse evidence as opposed to formative study days or certificated courses.

Even though governed by the HPC some groups also have their own professional body's requirements:

- *Occupational therapists* — their Code of Conduct states 'All occupational therapists shall be responsible for maintaining their evidence of their CPD'... and 'be accountable for the quality of their work and base this on current guidance, research, reasoning and the best available evidence'. (College of Occupational therapists 2005: 16).

- *Prosthetists and orthotists* — have added that, 'all members have the individual responsibility to maintain their level of professional competence and to be aware of current legal issues of practice'. (British Association of Prosthetists and Orthotists 2002: 12).
- *Optometrists* — the College of Optometrists (2007) and the Optical Council (which covers Optometrists and dispensing Opticians) added their own statement in relation to CPD stating that 'only by maintaining competence can practitioners individually continue to offer the best possible service to the public' (COP 2007: 01.01.1).

Other professional bodies in their codes such as the Arts Therapists (2005) and Sports Therapist (2005) just use the HPC standards.

Some other professional groups not covered by the HPC include:

- *Nurses and midwives* — whose Code of Professional Conduct (NMC, 2008) states that nurses and midwives must keep skills and knowledge up to date.
- *Vascular technologists* — the Society for Vascular Technology of Great Britain and Ireland (2007) in section 6, states that 'members must maintain and develop their professional knowledge and competence'.
- *Dentists and dental assistants* — in 2002 the General Dental Council introduced compulsory CPD for all dental professionals (GDC 2008). This symbolized a growing recognition for ways to further support their professional development. They require evidence that dental practitioners are keeping up to date with changes and require them to demonstrate this through their practice. They suggest this can be obtained through activities such as study, training courses, seminars, reading and other activities, which could reasonably be expected to advance their development as dental professionals (GDC 2008). They state that there should be up to 100 hours over a five-year period for the non-verifiable element of the CPD and 150 hours has to be verifiable and supported with certificated learning. The Royal College of Surgeons of England, Faculty of Dental Surgery suggest that the surgeons should have 250 hours over a five year period and this was compulsory CPD for all dental professionals in 2008.
- *Doctors* — the General Medical Council in their document *Protecting Patients and Guiding Doctors* (2004) states that 'CPD allows doctors to demonstrate that they are maintaining their skills in practice. It allows doctors to develop professionally and learn from more informal experiences....' (GMC 2004: 3). The actual requirements are set out by the Federation of Royal College of Physicians who use a credit-based system stating that each doctor should obtain 50 credits per year with

25 of those gained externally and up to 10 can be personal. The Royal College of Surgeons of England states that they have 250 hours over a five year period.

- *Counsellors and psychotherapists* – produced their *Ethical Framework for Good Practice* in 2002 with standards for CPD (British Association for Counselling and Psychotherapy 2002).
- *Other professional groups* — although we have noted some healthcare professionals, most professional groups such as teachers, police, lawyers and business managers are expected, by their professional bodies, to complete CPD. We could go on with other professional groups that have produced Codes of Conducts and guidelines for CPD. However from the selection we can see how they all place value on CPD and its relationship to quality care provision.

Joint statements by professional bodies

A joint statement, in relation to CPD, was published and included the Royal College of Nursing, Institute of Biomedical Science, Unison, British Academy of Audiology, Royal College of Midwives, the British Association of Arts Therapists, Allied Health Professional Forum Scotland, Allied Health Professions Federation, the British Dietetic Association, the British Association of Dramatherapists, the College of Occupational Therapists, the British Association of Prosthetists and Orthotists, the Royal College of Speech and Language Therapists, the Society of Chiropodists and Podiatrists, the Society of Radiographers, the British Paramedic Association College of Paramedics and the Chartered Society of Physiotherapists.

> *All these governing bodies have come together to state their commitment to continuing professional development and included in their statements that it is 'fundamental to the development of all health and social care practitioners, and to enhance the patient/client care within uni and multi professional teams.*

(Royal College of Nursing 2007: 2)

Governmental requirements

We have noted above what some of the professional bodies requirements are in relation to continuing professional development for the practising professional, however now we need to put that into context with Government requirements. The Darzi Report (DH 2008) clearly notes the importance of

CPD for a quality-focused patient-centred and clinically-driven approach to care. This follows a series of other reports such as *A First Class Service: Quality in the New NHS* (DH 1999), *Improving Working Lives Standard* (DH 2000), *NHS Knowledge and Skills Framework* (DH 2004) and *Learning from Tragedy* (DH 2007). All of the documents note the importance of professionals maintaining and developing their professional competence in order to provide a quality service. Only the KSF document sets out additional statutary requirements for professionals working within the NHS.

Tensions in relation to CPD

Although we note the legal and professional obligation for CPD above, attempting to maintain these requirements can result in tensions between the individual practitioner, the professional body and the employer, especially with those professional bodies who note specific timing and credits to obtain. Tensions might arise between individuals who aim to maintain their registration and the employer's commitment to development. Or there may be a mismatch between individual professional goals and organizational goals or personal ambitions and employer support or demands. These mismatches can result in a negative perception of individuals about employers' support for their CPD, leading to some tensions between the two (Munro 2008). The Darzi Report (DH 2008) goes some way to acknowledging this and aims to rate employers on their provision and commitment through CPD, making the process more visible with some accountability being placed on the employer.

Gaining CPD in the workplace through reflection

As stated, CPD is not a luxury but a statutory requirement for all professional practitioners as well as other healthcare workers within the NHS. As professionals we also have a personal goal to maintain standards and provide the best possible quality care to those we work for and with. However, reading through some of the definitions for gaining that development there are some vague statements in relation to the actual requirements other than time factors.

Learning from practice, we can not only achieve these statutory requirements for the profession and employer, but also we can gain personal satisfaction in the care we provide. Therefore reflection can help us not only to move that practice forward, to relate the theory to practice, but also, if recorded, can provide evidence that can be bought forward to meet the KSF and Statutory requirements for registration for the respective professional governing body.

In *Chapter 3* we note how we can learn directly from our patients/clients. Recording these learning experiences and incidents provides valuable evidence of learning from practice (Ghaye and Lillyman 2006). Please remember this does not have to be a negative experience, as noted in *Chapter 1*, but can be based on positive practice and is a chance to celebrate that practice.

In this book we want to encourage professional practitioners to take on board some of the aspects of reflection that can be related to their own professional development, as we note in the first principle of reflection it is about you and your work. The other eleven principles will guide you through different aspects of reflection and ultimately how reflection can improve practice through a systematic and rigorous approach to CPD.

References

British Association for Counselling and Psychotherapy (2002) *Ethical framework for good practice in counselling and psychotherapy.* British Association for Counselling and Psychotherapy. London

British Association of Prothetists and Orthotists. (2002) *The Ethical Code for Prothetists and Orthotists.* British Association of Prothetists and Orthotists, London.

College of Occupational Therapists (2005) *Code of Ethics and Professional Conduct.* College of Occupational Therapists London

College of Optometrists (2007) *Code of Ethics and Guidelines for Professional Conduct.* College of Optometrists. London

Department of Health. (1999) *A First Class Service: quality in the new NHS.* The stationary office, London

Department of Health (2000) *Improving working lives standard.* The stationary office, London

Department of Health. (2004) *The NHS Knowledge and Skills Framework (NHS KSF) and the Development Review Process.* The Stationary Office, London

Department of Health. (2007) *Learning from Tragedy, keeping patients safe.* The stationary office, London

Department of Health. (2008) *A High Quality Workforce; NHS next stage review.* Department of Health, London.

Department of Health. (2009) *A High Quality Care for All; The Journey so far.* Department of Health, London.

Ghaye T and Lillyman S (2006) *Learning Journals and Critical Incidents end edition.* Mark Allen Publishing Salisbury.

General Dental Council (2008) *The General Dental Council (Continuing Professional Development)* (Dentists rules order of council 2008). GDC, London

General Medical Council (2004) *General Medical Council Protecting Patients and Guiding Doctors*. GMC, London.

Health Professional Council (2005) *Standards for Continuing Professional Development*. HPC, London

Health Professional Council (2008) *Your duties as a registrant. Your guide to our standards for continuing professional development*. HPC, London

Munro K (2008) Continuing professional development and the charity paradigm: Interrelated individual, collective and organizational issues about continuing professional development. *Nurse Education Today* **28**, 953-961

Nursing and Midwifery Council (2008) *Code of Professional Conduct*. NMC. London.

Royal college of Nursing (2007) *Joint position statement. A joint statement on continuing professional development for health and social care practitioners*. RCN, London

The British Association of Art Therapists Ltd (2005) *Code of Ethics and Principles of practice for Art Therapists*. The British Association of Art Therapists Ltd, London

The Society of Sports Therapists. (2009) *Standards of Conduct, performance and Ethics*. The Society of Sports Therapists. London

The Society of Vascular Technology of Great Britain and Ireland (2007) *Continuing Professional development for accreditation for clinical vascular scientists*. The Society of Vascular Technology of Great Britain and Ireland. London

CHAPTER 8

Reflections on practice: Magic moments and moving forward

In stating Principle 4 (*reflective practice is about learning how to account positively for ourselves*) we were implying that we should take some responsibility for our own future clinical and professional development. Dewey (1933) had much to say about responsibility. He saw it as an attribute of reflective practitioners.

Some reflections on Dewey

One restricted interpretation of this is to say that 'responsible' action is when clinicians ask themselves why they are doing what they are doing. Dewey (1933) extends this. Essentially, for him, it was about the consequences of the acts of practice. He regarded responsibility as being prepared to consider what is worthwhile in an 'educative' relationship (he was referring to teachers and children). Applied to healthcare, this means that responsible action is more than just considering 'what works' for me, or for us, right now, just here. It involves a reflection on both the means and the ends of the caring process or 'pathway'. Dewey also talked about open-mindedness and whole-heartedness as other essential attributes of reflective practitioners. The first is about reflecting-on-action, confronting those values upon which our practice (and the practice of others) is predicated, and being 'open' to other possibilities. It is a particular kind of reflection which we have called '*receptive reflection-on-action*' (see *Chapter 5*). Whole-heartedness, for Dewey, is about being energetic and enthusiastic and about approaching our work in a frame of mind which accepts that there is always something new to be learned every time we are at work. Reflective practice, then, is a combination of a disposition towards our work (a frame of mind, or mind-set) together with understanding, embracing and utilizing a set of principles and skills. Taken together, these equip us to study our clinical actions and provide the opportunity for us to become even better at what we do, over time. This assumption of responsibility is a central feature of the idea of the reflective practitioner (Zeichner and Liston 1996). All this prepares the way for the tenth principle of reflective practice, which is:

Principle 10: Reflection can improve practice

The healthcare literature is increasingly having to acknowledge the benefits for clinicians from learning through reflection, although much more work needs to be reported on the impact of reflective practitioners on the management of care, as experienced through the reports of patients, clients and colleagues. We have been suggesting throughout this book that reflection-on-practice helps us to make wise and principled clinical and professional decisions. We do this by developing individual and collective 'knowledges' which enable us to 'see through' clinical situations, to develop better understandings of them and to make commitments to improve them. Engaging in the processes of reflection which we are advocating means admitting that practice can always be improved in some way. We need to nourish the 'good bits' and devise ways of tackling the 'messy bits'. Reflection-on-practice refuses to let experience become a liability. As we said in explaining Principle 2 (*reflective practice is about learning from experience*), reflection takes experience and re-frames the problematic aspects of it so that it becomes workable. Reflection helps to establish the improvement agenda for individuals and groups. It can provide us with the courage and intellectual capacity to turn insight into improved action. With the appropriate blend of structure, support and challenge, the reflective process provides opportunities for moving thinking and clinical action forward. In an important sense, reflection has a creative quality to it. But it needs to be done by socially committed individuals and clinical teams.

A few words of caution. Reflection-on-practice is a complex process. We have argued throughout this book that it symbolizes much more than merely 'thinking about what we do', and we have learned that it is not a 'toolbox' of methods and 'tricks of the trade'. This would be a very impoverished view of reflective practice. It is rather a blend of practice with principle. It is not always 'safe' and can, indeed, be threatening as one questions one's practice. It is about being professionally self-critical without being destructive and overly negative. It is not something to be 'bolted-on' to courses and programmes of study. We do not believe you can profess to being a reflective practitioner for one day a week and some kind of healthcare worker for the rest. It is not something you can 'commodify'; just pick up and put down, buy into or not, almost at will.

Getting the most from reflective practice means having a consistently reflective approach to our work. As Dewey (1933) said, 'It is a whole way of being'. It is not self-indulgent 'navel-gazing'. Neither is it a process of self-victimization and self-destruction. Reflection-on-practice should not be support without challenge, for this might be a bit like having a warm bath or wrapping ourselves up in a comfort blanket. Seeing reflection-on-practice as support can serve certain purposes. It can also be justified in certain circumstances. Street (1995) calls this 'the tyranny of niceness'. Alternatively, the reflective process should not be all challenge without support, for this can prove demoralizing. Placed in the 'wrong hands' reflective practices are dangerous. With inexperienced facilitators it can be embarrassing or worse, uncovering and disclosing issues and concerns which those taking part may be ill-equipped to handle. Ideally, reflective practices need to be a judicious blend of sensitive support, appropriate structure and constructive challenge.

Who owns the improvement process?

Throughout this book we have stressed the personal and collective commitment we need to have to get the most from reflective practice. We have also tried to persuade you to value the personal-practical knowledge which reflection generates. Implicit within these two statements is the issue of 'ownership'. If we have no stake in the knowledge generated through reflection (or by any other means for that matter), then how can we always feel committed to it, believe in it and get the most from it? The issue of ownership and how this links with Dewey's notion of responsible action mentioned earlier, is well illustrated, for example, in a series of short reflective accounts written up by the South West Wirral elderly mental health community team (Rushton et al 1999). One of the accounts (we thank the whole team for allowing us to share their work) is presented here:

Falling asleep

Each visit is a new event. Something will have changed. Nothing ever remains the same. This is what I tell myself as I prepare to visit one of my long-standing regular clients, Miss Jones. Miss Jones lives alone in a small bungalow. A home help comes in every day and she also gets help from neighbours and employs a jobbing gardener to attend to house repairs and maintain the neat front and rear gardens. The house is always neat and tidy, but the atmosphere is somewhat oppressive.

Miss Jones has a long history of schizo-affective disorder with paranoid ideation. This had been controlled with oral medication for many years without problems, but nine months previously she began to suffer severe tardive dyskinesia, which affected her limbs and facial nerves, and this was when I was asked to visit.

We have managed to control the symptoms by careful balancing of her medication over a two-month period, but I continue to visit. I rationalise these visits as necessary to supervise and monitor her medication, but in fact it's more that Miss Jones' physical health is deteriorating. She can no longer get out much and she is clearly feeling isolated and lonely.

But on the three times I have visited recently, I have fallen asleep! I have excuses. Miss Jones' long, drawn-out, repetitive monologues, which tend to tell the same story, regardless of the opening topic; lack of oxygen in the over-heated room; overwork and plain tiredness. But it is inexcusable to nod off during a visit to a client.

REFLECTION: I must try to control our conversations more and focus on the mental health aspects. If (when) I realize I am clouding over, I should tell her and go out for some fresh air. I am bored because I allow Miss Jones to keep telling me the same story. I should challenge her more and be a little more dynamic in my approach. I must prepare myself more before the visit.

Engagement in the improvement process means that reflective practitioners need to embrace the 'strategic action' intention of action research (McMahon 1999). In other words, we are arguing that reflection is not simply (and only) about identifying 'problems'. The strategic intent of some kinds of reflection (see *Chapter 5*) is to do something about them. To clarify the point further: not all kinds of reflection are committed to improving practice. Some kinds, such as descriptive reflections-on-practice, are more committed to presenting, disclosing and understanding a particular concern more richly and deeply. Other kinds of reflection, particularly what we have called creative-critical and interactive reflections-on-practice, are indeed imbued with this strategic intent, to improve practice in a systematic and rigorous manner. We do not agree, therefore, with Schön who described reflection as 'non-rigorous inquiry' (Schön 1987: 3). It is necessary for reflective practitioners to learn from action researchers. The two have much to share and there is much to gain from collaborating. One can be a reflective practitioner but not an action researcher. Action researchers, by their very nature, would feel comfortable with many of the principles of reflective practice described in this book.

How far is reflective practice educative?

Just as there are different types of research, generated in different ways to serve different needs, so too are there different types of reflection which serve different interests. One of the main reasons for engaging in reflective practice is to get some kind of improvement in our thinking about our clinical/professional/managerial work, our practice itself and/or the context in which the two are embedded. Reflection is about generating personal-practical knowledge and learning from it. Because improvement is a very value-laden word (we do not all agree what improvement looks like) and knowledge is uncertain and provisional (see *Chapter 3*), reflection becomes vital in reviewing and reappraising the clinical and educative potency of reflective practice. In Dewey's (1933) spirit of open-mindedness, reflective practitioners need to be prepared to seek out alternative views on things (receptive reflection-on-action) and to be open to other viewpoints. In this way we continue to deepen our individual and collective understandings.

Reflective practice is educative practice. In the following list, we have adapted the qualities of 'educative research' (Gitlin and Russell 1994) to illustrate this important attribute of reflective practice for healthcare professionals. In our view, reflective practice can be called 'educative' because it:

- encourages us to work together to jointly negotiate and attribute meaning to what it is we are reflecting upon
- acknowledges that the focus of reflection (the concern) has to be understood in its particular historical, cultural and organizational context
- encourages clinicians to ask questions and engage in reflective conversations about practice
- tries to question both the ordinary and the extraordinary aspects of practice,
- gives a voice to practitioners themselves as they try to make sense of uncertainty and the internal and external influences which serve to liberate or constrain what they do, and of alternative ways of doing things
- is an ongoing learning process where new sensitivities and skills are progressively developed and re-interpreted
- places healthcare professionals in the centre of their own actions and accounts of practice, thus giving reflective accounts their own value-laden character and authenticity
- has a particular view of valid and reliable accounts from reflective

practitioners. The validity of a reflective account is arrived at through dialogue and mutual understanding, and from listening to and challenging participant views and positions. Reliability is linked to the importance of the voice of the clinician in his or her own clinical area. It is often both undesirable and inappropriate for the reflective process to remain unchanged from clinical area to clinical area. What is important is that the process is justified in relation to the clinical concern, those involved and the purpose and interests that reflection is serving.

The reflective practitioner-researcher: juggling roles

Earlier we suggested that reflective practice might usefully be seen as a disposition towards practice (a whole way of being, a frame of mind or mind-set). Part of this disposition is viewing practice through a 'research lens'. Research does not have to be known and understood as something mysterious and done by those 'out there' (although undoubtedly much of it still is). Research can be done by us, in our own clinical contexts, in our own 'customized' and justified manner. So in this section we want to introduce the eleventh principle of reflective practice, which is:

> **Principle 11:** Reflective practitioners develop themselves and their work systematically and rigorously

The idea of educare professionals (such as nurses, teachers, social workers) viewing themselves as researchers in their own work settings, emanates principally from education and the pioneering work of Stenhouse (1975, 1983). Of particular relevance to this book are the ideas that we:

- should regard ourselves as researchers-in-practice
- need to reflect critically and systematically on our practice
- should have a commitment to question our practice and that this should form the basis of development
- should have the commitment and skills to study our own practice and, in so doing, develop the art of self-study
- might benefit from our work being observed by others and then discussing it with them in an open and honest manner
- should have a concern to question and to test theory-in-practice.

The Stenhouse view of research is very relevant to our view of reflective practitioners. In fact, it is arguably one of the distinguishing qualities of such people. He saw research as a public activity, as systematic and sustained enquiry, planned and self-critical. He argued that if we were to develop our practice and our understandings of the links between practice and theory (see *Chapter 4*), we should be prepared to place our accounts in the public domain where they could be critiqued and perhaps utilized by others. This process of improvement was not viewed as a private act, solitary and introspective, but as a public and discursive one. This is supportive of the view of the reflective practitioner which we are advocating in this book.

The thrust of Stenhouse's work which is relevant to healthcare professionals is that:

- all our practice should be informed by a kind of practitioner-research
- the idea of practitioner-researchers, researching in their own clinical areas, supports, nourishes and extends our professionalism
- the idea of practitioner-researchers is an important element in the professionalism of healthcare workers
- the idea of practitioner-researchers can reinforce our sense of professional responsibility and autonomy.

Reflective action and active reflection: resolving caring concerns

In Ghaye et al (1996) we set out an argument for, and illustrated the notion of, research-based practice. In this chapter we only have space to make some general but important links with action research. Currently in healthcare work, an increasing number of practitioners are using forms of action research (Titchen and Binnie 2008, Kelly and Simpson 2008). Such nursing journals as *Nurse Researcher* are devoting special issues to it (for example, volume 16, number 2, 2009), and organizations such as the Royal College of Nursing hold annual conferences about it. The international Collaborative Action Research Network (CARN) has a healthcare sub-group.

In general terms Carr and Kemmis (1986: 162) define much of the character of action research when they say that it is a:

...form of self-reflective enquiry undertaken by practitioners in social situations in order to improve the rationality and justice of their own practices, their understanding of these practices, and the situations in which the practices are carried out... In terms of method, a self-reflective spiral of cycles of planning, acting, observing and reflecting is central to the action research approach.

For those in healthcare who are attracted to the natural affinity which reflection has with action research, the work of Kemmis and McTaggart (1988) which evolved from Lewin's earlier work (1946), is a good starting point. You can usually spot an action research account by the way it is organized as a series of action-reflection cycles (or spirals). Within each cycle/spiral there are four 'magic moments'. 'Magic' in the sense that at each part of the enquiry process there is an element of revelation and deeper insight. We come to know more about how to research the clinical/ professional/managerial concern and more about the nature of it. The four moments of action research are:

1. *Plan and re-plan*: We develop a plan (an action plan) with the intention of trying to improve what is already happening.
2. *Act*: We put the plan into action. We implement it.
3. *Observe*: We observe the effects of the action in the context in which it occurs.
4. *Reflect*: We reflect on the evidence we have gathered, we see what it tells us and, on the basis of this, we make judgements about what we can claim to know now and what to do next. This leads to a new plan.

These four moments are usually depicted as a spiral, not as a closed circle.

Action research, rather like reflective practice, can have both individual and collective dimensions. Henry (1991: 105–106) goes on to say:

> *One of the things that I now know, and should have known before but did not, is something about the relationship between knowledge and action... A key feature of action research... is one way in which it links action and understanding (theory and practice): acting on the world leads to better understanding of the world, and better understanding to more prudent action.*

In this interpretation, Henry uses the term 'change' rather than 'improvement'. We know that all change is not improvement. We also know, from clinical experience, that we sometimes have to change things (a directive, an imposition) and it is not until later that we find out how far the change might be called an improvement. Whitehead (1993) helps to pull together a number of the ideas we have expressed in *Chapter 6* and thus far in *Chapter 8*. He suggests that the improvement process might most usefully begin with a reflection on the negation of our values in practice, thus:

1. I experience a concern when some of my values are denied in my practice.
2. I imagine a solution to the concern.
3. I act in the direction of the solution.
4. I evaluate the solution.
5. I modify my practice in the light of the solution.

This is an extremely helpful framework for healthcare, and resonates with many of the principles of reflective practice which we have described. The emphasis on 'experiencing a concern' reminds us that we reflect upon that which we are (trying) to live out, that which we are 'living' through. 'Imagining a solution' is an invitation, through informed and committed actions, to be creative in trying to move practice forward. The next stage (3) is the strategic intent of action research. 'Evaluation' (stage 4) is really a collective noun for many things. It implies the gathering of, the making sense of evidence, and its public validation. The final phase (stage 5) reminds us of the things we have said earlier about the impact of personal-practical knowledge on our work.

The word 'impact' is becoming increasingly fashionable in healthcare, and certainly in the context of evidence-based practice (see *Chapter 9*). The impact of reflection on practice (whether we engage with the action research process or not) may be thought about as follows:

1. *No impact*: Findings, claims to know, discoveries ignored or not actioned.
2. *Self-transformative*: Big impact on me as the one at the centre of the reflective process.
3. *Transformative*: Impact on others and upon the context in which practice is embedded.
4. *Confrontational*: Provokes a reaction from others which may not result in some kind of improvement. This is part of the flip-side of reflection. Through the process and its public articulation we may reveal things which some would rather not know about. Sometimes we have to ride this one out. Sometimes things have to get worse before then can get better!

Moving forward: some reflective techniques

Reflective practice is not a collection of techniques alone. But techniques are needed to bring alive the principles we have been presenting to you. We shall briefly outline some of the relatively 'less technical' but none-the-less useful techniques which you might use. They all have both strengths and limitations. From a range of techniques which include visual art, poetry, music, critical shared reading, drama/role playing, peer observation, clinical supervision, action learning sets, and so on, we shall outline how you might use (mind) mapping, critical incident analysis, journal writing and storying as techniques.

Concept mapping

In the current context, a concept map (Ghaye and Lillyman 2006) contains healthcare knowledge represented in the form of a labelled line graph structure. The fundamental elements are:

- *Nodes*: These are key ideas or concepts which act as the catalyst for reflection.
- *Links*: These are the lines we draw between the nodes. They do not have to be straight ones. We can draw on to the paper as many links as we can, or wish to, given the time available.
- *Labels*: These are what we choose to write on each link. This turns the 'map' into a labelled-line map. It is important to label each link so that the way you are linking them up in your mind becomes more public and therefore more knowable. In this way, each map becomes a personal reality map, constructed by you (individually or with others) to express the sense you are currently making of a particular facet of your work.

Try to think of five or six key ideas to act as the building blocks for the map. These can be personally arrived at, or jointly through team discussion. The ideas can be quite concrete or more abstract ones depending on the purpose of the exercise and the participants involved. For example, from a group of 10 school nurses who were discussing ways of working more collaboratively in school, the following six ideas were jointly derived and then acted on as the basis for the group's mapping exercise. The ideas were: school nurse, child/children, teachers, family, collaboration and reflection. For a group of eight experienced nurses undertaking a Masters degree in clinical nursing, and a module called Advancing Nursing Practice, the following ideas were used: advancing nursing, resistance, identity, workplace, opportunity, and reflection. Time needs to be given over to the choice of ideas. Each one needs a justification for inclusion in the exercise. It is interesting how different each map can be. Maps can therefore be used to facilitate reflective conversations about practice. The similarities and differences between maps can be explored. Actions can be planned; multiple and constructed realities discussed. Concept mapping embraces many of the principles of reflective practice in one exercise.

Critical (or significant) incident analysis

This is another popular technique. Tripp (1993: 8) defines critical incidents thus:

> *... incidents happen, but critical incidents are produced by the way we look at a situation, it is an interpretation of the significance of the event.*

In Ghaye and Lillyman (2006) we wrote that critical incidents do not have to be those of an 'emergency' nature, such as a cardiac arrest or a drug error. Critical incident analysis (CIA) begins by finding something significant, from practice, to reflect upon in a systematic manner. The actual incident may be ordinary — not necessarily extraordinary — something that went particularly well, or where values were negated in practice, an incident from which we feel more might be learned, and so on. It does not have to be something that is worrying us, or that went wrong (although many choose incidents like this).

There are a number of ways in which the incident can now be analysed. Tripp (1993), Lillyman and Evans (1996) and Lillyman (2000) suggest, for example, that we analyse the incident by asking questions about it, particularly 'why-type' questions and questions which get us to look at the incident in other ways. Another method is to search out and try to understand the 'dilemmas' present in the practice incident, for example as evident in the lack of congruence between what we say and do. Above all else, CIA is a reflective learning technique. It can help us to appreciate those aspects of our practice which may lie hidden and uncelebrated. The learning can be used to fulfil post-registration education and practice (PREP) requirements and can add fuel to the argument that healthcare needs to be evidence-based.

Journal writing (learning journals, learning logs)

In Paterson (1995), Ghaye and Lillyman (2006), Riley-Doucet and Wilson (1997) we find answers to the common questions asked about journal writing. These are: 'Why do I need/should I keep a journal?', 'What might I write in it?', 'How often do I make entries in it?' and 'What are the likely benefits and difficulties if I try to keep one?' With this technique (as with the others) there are a certain number of ethical issues to be resolved, and a code of practice to be established. For example, there is the issue of 'rights'. Who has the right to decide what is written and shared? Is it wise to assume that we have the right to keep what is written private and confidential? What happens if journal writing gets to be part of some kind of assessment process for a course? Tied with this is the issue of consent: in journal writing, who is telling what, to whom and why? This needs to be sorted out. There are risks and benefits associated with this technique. The benefits are linked to all those things we have said about learning from experience. Some of the risks are to do with the making of entries in a context of increasing personal accountability, defamation and litigation. Questions such as, 'How far is the account true?', 'How far are we sure of it?' and 'What are the risks associated with not being sure?' need to be asked and responded to (Theobold 1995).

Storying

In the literature on reflective practice we always see reference being made to reflection as a way of turning experience into learning (Pierson 1998). It is our second principle. But experience can also turn into stories. Over time, stories transform into experience. Experience is a private thing. To make it public, and therefore to add value to it by reflecting (again) upon it, we have to find some means of representing it. In Ghaye and Lillyman (2000) we have edited a book of powerful caring stories. By telling each other stories about practice, we give ourselves opportunities to make more sense of our work. Stories have to be analysed in some manner. Once the story is written/ told we can then make a prudent decision with regard to which model of reflection (and there are many!) we might use to help us to make sense of the account. Of course, we do not have to turn to a 'model'. The attributes of a reflective conversation (see *Chapter 5*) might be used to guide our individual thinking or group dialogues.

How can I improve my practice here?

Diversity of purpose and approach are both aspects of improving practice. It is therefore our belief that we should not be prescriptive in outlining how you might improve your own practice. However, for those wishing to embrace Principles 10 and 11, we suggest that you consider asking yourself the following reflective questions. They may act as useful focusing and filtering devices; as ways of enabling you to confront yourself and the context in which you work; and as a means by and through which you can develop a creative response to improving your practice. You might ask yourself:

- What is my/our practice like?
- Why is it like this?
- How has it come to be this way?

- What aspects of it would I/we like to improve? (Be realistic!)
- How far do I/we live my/our values out in my/our caring work?
- How far does the culture of my/our workplace help or hinder this?
- Whose interests are being served or denied by my/our practice?
- What internal conditions nourish or constrain my/our practice?
- What external pressures prevent/limit me/us from working in alternative ways?
- What alternatives are available to me/us right now?

Out of this questioning posture will come evidence, in one form or another, which will need to be 'handled' and potentially learned from. Currently, evidence-based healthcare is a very 'hot' issue, closely linked to clinical effectiveness and value-for-money (cost-effectiveness) initiatives (CSAG, 1998). It is getting to be a bit of a buzz word, especially in the context of clinical governance. In essence, evidence-based healthcare is about policy and practice being justified in relation to the 'best' evidence that is available to us, evidence that we can understand and do something with. We can both generate and consume evidence. This leads us to the twelfth principle of reflective practice, which is:

Principle 12: Reflection involves respecting and working with evidence

It is necessary for reflective practitioners to be fully committed to developing reflective-conversational communities. Although we know that the building of such communities is a daunting task, it is nevertheless a vital one if we are to develop a culture where evidence which substantiates the claims we wish to make, is valued over opinion. In such communities, for example, in naturally occurring clinical teams, multi-disciplinary or inter-agency teams, clinical supervision teams, and so on, there is an opportunity to reflect on practice and to critically review, re-see and reconstruct what we do through evidence-based dialogue. When reflective practitioners talk about what they have learned and the consequences of this, a question which constantly needs to be asked is, 'What kind of evidence have you got to support what it is you now claim to know and wish to do?' Safe and accountable practice is evidence-based. Reflective practitioners are respectful of this. By implication, then, 'moving forward' must be based upon some kind of evidence. The generation and the use of evidence by healthcare professionals, in the way we have been advocating, can be described as 'magical moments' as new sensitivities and opportunities reveal themselves.

References

Carr W, Kemmis S (1986) *Becoming Critical: Education, Knowledge and Action Research*. The Falmer Press, London

Clinical Standards Advisory Group (CSAG) (1998) *Clinical Effectiveness*. HMSO, London

Dewey J (1933) *How we Think: A restatement ofthe relation of reflective thinking to the educative process*. Henry Regnery Publishers, Chicago

Ghaye T, et al (1996) *Research-Based Practice; Resolving Care Problems, Learning Through Critical Reflective Practice: Self-supported Learning Experiences for Healthcare Professionals*. Pentaxion Press, Newcastle upon Tyne

Ghaye T, Lillyman S (2006) *Learning Journals and Critical Incidents: Reflective Practice for Healthcare Professionals*. 2nd edition. Mark Allen Publishers, Salisbury

Ghaye T, Lillyman S (2000) *Caring Moments: The Discourse of Reflective Practice*. Mark Allen Publishing, Salisbury

Gitlin A, Russell R (1994) Alternative methodologies and the research context. In: Gitlin A ed. *Power and Method: Political Activism and Educational Research*. Routledge, London

Henry C (1991) Reflections at the End of the Congress: If Action Research were Tennis. in Zuber-skerritt O, ed (1991) *Action Learning for improved performance*. AEBIS Publishing, Brisbane

Kelly D and Simpson S (2008) Action research in action: reflections on a project to introduce clinical practice facilitators to an acute hospital setting. *Journal of Advanced Nursing* **33**(5) 652-659

Kemmis S, McTaggart R (1988) *The Action Research Planner*. Deakin University Press, Geelong, South Australia

Lewin K (1946) Action research and minority problems. *J Social Issues* **2**: 34–46

Lillyman S (2000) Critical incidents as caring moments. In: Ghaye T, Lillyman S eds. *Caring Moments: The Discourse of Reflective Practice*. Mark Allen Publishing, Salisbury

Lillyman S, Evans B (1996) *Designing a Personal Portfolio/Profile: A workbookfor healthcare professionals*. Quay Books, Mark Allen Publishing, Salisbury

McMahon T (1999) Is reflective practice synonymous with action research? *Educational Action Res* **J7**(1): 163–8

Paterson B (1995) Developing and maintaining reflection in clinical journals. *Nurse Educ Today* **15**: 120–121

Pierson W (1998) Reflection and nursing education. *J Adv Nurs* **27**: 165–70

Riley-Doucet C, Wilson S (1997) A three-step method of self-reflection using reflective journal writing. *J Adv Nurs* **25**: 964–8

Rushton B et al (1999) Pause for Thought. *Mental Health Care* 2(8): 277–9

Schön D (1987) *Educating the Reflective Practitioner.* Jossey Bass, San Francisco

Stenhouse L (1975) *An introduction to curriculum research and development.* Heinemann, London

Stenhouse L (1983) *Authority, Education and Emancipation.* Educational Books, London

Street J (1995) *Nursing Replay: Researching Nursing Culture Together.* Churchill Livingstone, Australia

Street A, Robinson A (1994) Advanced clinical roles: investigating dilemmas and changing practice through action research. *J Clin Nurs* 4: 349–57

Theobold M (1995) The nature of nursing knowledge. Keynote speech at the RCN conference on Reflective Practice: The Impact on Patient Care. The Commonwealth Institute, London

Titchen a and Binnie A (2008) Research Partnerships, collaborative research in Nursing. *Journal of Advanced Nursing* 18(6) 858-865

Tripp D (1993) *Critical incidents in teaching.* Routledge, London

Whitehead J (1993) *The Growth of Educational Knowledge: Creating your own living educational theories.* Hyde Publications, Bournemouth

Zeichner K, Liston D (1996) *Reflective Teaching: An Introduction.* Lawrence Erlbaum Associates, New Jersey

CHAPTER 9

Reflections on context: Towards the reflective organization

Our values make us the kind of healthcare workers that we are. We have argued that we should try to make deliberate, conscious and sincere attempts to live our values out in our caring work. We have also made the point that this is not always possible. One of the major influences here is the 'culture' of the workplace. This serves both to liberate and to constrain us. It provides opportunities for achieving satisfaction, personal renewal and collective (team) regeneration. Workplace culture can also stifle, suffocate, marginalize and silence its workers. Critical reflection-on-practice questions and confronts those things which 'disempower' and demoralise us.

The link between the quality of our caring work and the workplace culture is a vast and complicated subject. All we can do here is to indicate what we believe are five of the things we might usefully consider if we have a commitment to move from being the individual reflective practitioner, through building and working in reflective teams, towards developing the reflective organization (Ghaye 2008). The first thing to consider is the 'reflection gap'.

Reflecting on the 'reflection gap'

In times of rapid and uncertain change in the NHS, there is an even greater requirement for reflection. A reflection gap:

> ...develops if people do not in fact become more reflective. This reflection gap will limit the possibilities for genuine enthusiasm and commitment.
> (Senge et al 1999: 198)

We need to reflect upon the extent to which our own (individual and team) values join up with organizational values. We might also reflect on the extent to which those initiating or imposing change are trustworthy and respected, especially if they are in positions of authority. Reflections of this kind can only take place in a context of mutual respect, with an acknowledgement of difference and safety. The interplay between reflection, values and trust is a key component of developing a reflective organization.

> *In traditional work environments, you needed to understand the job, you needed to understand the business goals, you needed to understand the political environment you were operating in, but you really didn't need to understand what you stood for. In the new type of organization we are now creating, 'knowing what you stand for' is a crucial first step in defining your relationship with your bosses and subordinates, your conception of your work, and your role in the enterprise around you.*
> (Senge et al 1999: 199)

Having the curiosity and courage to question practice

Earlier in this book (in *Chapter 3*) we discussed the issue of knowledge production and use, and addressed the question, 'What knowledge is worth knowing?' Tied up in this discussion was the link between knowledge and power. In a 'spoken' book, Paulo Freire and his colleague Antonio Faundez engage in a reflective conversation about learning to question. Paulo says:

> ... *the problem facing us today... is not that of simply gaining power but... creating a new power which does not fear to be called in question and does not become rigid....* .
> (Freire and Faundez 1989: 2)

We call the knowledge we use in our caring work into question by reflecting on its relevance and meaningfulness in helping us work safely and accountably. But in order to reflect we have to be curious.

Curiosity fuels the reflective process. We have argued throughout that the personal-practical knowledge which reflection can produce begins with asking questions. Some of these are set out clearly in *Chapters 1 and 5*. Asking a 'good' reflective question is a skilful business.

Once asked, we should then explore it in the spirit of reflective action. Knowledge for safe and accountable practice does not come ready made. We need to create and recreate it through a continuous cycle of reflection-action-reflection. In reflective organizations, asking questions is encouraged. The challenge implicit in a question is not seen as an attack on authority but as a way of fulfilling our:

- moral obligation to serve the interests of our patients/clients and to decide how quality care can be fostered and promoted
- professional obligation to review periodically the nature and effectiveness of our practice in order to improve it
- professional obligation to continue to develop our practical knowledge both by personal reflection and through interaction with others. (adapted from Eraut 1995)

Reflective organizations respect our right to ask questions.

Caring for others but also caring for ourselves

In reflective organizations there is a consideration of both individual and collective values, and the ways in which these are lived out in practice (actions or behaviours). With this sort of consideration, the significance of the values which underpin practice can be constantly reviewed. Promoting values which help us to care for ourselves is a quality of a reflective organization. As Wright (1998: 180) suggests, we should take time to care for ourselves:

> *Nothing is so important that it burns you out, drains you completely, or destroys your valued relationships.*

These values are to do with 'affectivity' and connected relationships and receptivity and empathetic behaviour. They are the kind of values which emphasize collaboration rather than competition. They try to promote success and 'best' practice in the many, rather than simply promoting the successes of the few. In reflective organizations, building and nurturing meaningful relationships is a high, not a low-status activity. Such organizations try to look after the emotional needs of their workforces, attempting to make all their employees feel secure, happy and cared for, despite the relentless intensification of caseloads and the resultant administration, budget cuts, lack of career prospects, poor physical working conditions and the like. Developing reflective organizations is some task!

Joining up organizational effectiveness with organizational improvement

Earlier we spoke about clinical and cost-effectiveness in the contexts of clinical governance and evidence-based healthcare. Effectiveness and improvement are not synonymous, but they are linked. We can have improvement towards effectiveness and effectiveness that leads to some improvement. An important part of organizational effectiveness is mainly determined by clinical effectiveness. This brings the 'quality of caring' into the centre of the improvement process. The way individuals and clinical teams discharge their roles and responsibilities is a very important variable in the determination of effectiveness. But our roles and responsibilities change. We therefore need improvement strategies which keep us up-to-date and competent. Improvement is not merely an 'object', but rather a process, and a very complex, time-consuming and non-linear one which goes on at different levels within a healthcare organization. Knowledge about effectiveness helps us to plan for improvement. It tells us what is conditional for it to improve.

We seem to be back again to the question about 'knowledge creation'. Reflective organizations actively try to join up evidence about effectiveness with organizational improvement practices. They reflect on the way the one informs and transforms the other. Reflective organizations are certainly 'learning organizations' (Argyris 1999) in that they are about acquiring new, 'better' and more useful knowledge. But they do not see knowledge as a 'commodity', as a product. Reflective organizations spend time in knowledge creation. The role of reflective practice is fundamental here. Fullan (1999: 15–16) takes us back into our earlier discussions about the role of reflection in knowledge creation and, specifically, in making the 'tacit' more explicit (see *Chapters 4 and 5*):

> *In brief, the secret to success of living companies, complex adaptive systems, learning communities or whatever terms we wish to use, is that they consist of intricate, embedded interaction inside and outside the organization which converts tacit knowledge to explicit knowledge on an on-going basis... The process of knowledge creation is no easy task.*

Reflective organizations develop through empowerment

We have devoted a whole book in this series to empowerment (Ghaye, Gillespie and Lillyman 2000). Like some of the other terms we have used, there is much trumpet blowing and flag waving associated with empowerment. As with reflective practice, we should not celebrate empowerment uncritically (Jack 1995, Kendall 1998). In reflective organizations there is a commitment to develop through a view of empowerment which is about 'individuals and groups coming to know, express and critically analyse their own realities and having the commitment, will and power to act to transform these realities to enhance personal and collective well-being, security, satisfaction, capability and working conditions' (Ghaye, Gillespie and Lillyman 2000). In relation to developing through empowerment, the three points set out by Blanchard et al (1999) are important:

1. *Reflective organizations have a commitment to share information effectively:* In the spirit of our first principle (*reflective practice is about you and your work*), reflective organizations do not begin by 'chief executives' sharing their visions; they begin 'where we are at'. They begin with careful, curious and critical reflections on what they currently do. Reflective practitioners 'go public' on what they come to know. People without information cannot possibly act responsibly, safely and accountably.

2. *Reflective organizations create autonomy through new boundaries:* Reflective organizations are not governed by suffocating, hierarchical, command-and-control type structures. Perhaps this is one reason why so few exist!
   Within reflective organizations there emerges a new type of structure which is principally intended to inform workers about the ranges within which they can act with autonomy. The role of the reflective team (Andersen 1991) plays an important part in setting these boundaries which may express themselves in team goals, decision-making rules, protocols, and so on.

   Within the ranges set by those boundaries, team members can determine what to do and how to do it. As the empowerment process unfolds, the range of structures can widen and deepen to allow people greater degrees of control and responsibility.
   (Blanchard et al 1999: 11–12)

3. *Reflective teams become the 'hierarchy' in reflective organizations:* Reflective organizations are characterized by creative and critically reflective, self-directing teams which need to be nurtured and developed over time. These reflective teams make and implement decisions and are accountable for their performance (effectiveness). Senior managers, chief executives and trust boards need to learn how to work with (and learn from) these high performing reflective teams.

Much of what we have said here about moving from the individual to the organizational level, about teams, about improvement processes, structures and boundaries is summed up in the reflective notes of an experienced clinician working in a large children's hospital. After a day spent collaboratively exploring some principles and practices of reflection, she wrote:

This session really 'switched on the light' for me in terms of my understanding of reflective practice. Previously I had viewed reflective practice as a useful tool for personal development at a 'micro' level. I now realize this is a fairly narrow view. The possibility of harnessing reflective practice through multi-disciplinary reflective teams to create a real force for change is an exciting concept.

I now see reflective practice as a process for changing the way we work, through examining practice in a structured, systematic and analytical way. The best way to achieve this is probably through multi-disciplinary reflective teams, with the patient as a focus. By examining issues from the perspective of different professionals, a more holistic view of care can be achieved. It is important that individuals and teams are equipped with the principles and skills of reflection...

The impact of the context in which we work, on how we work, is important to understand. Reflective practice will thrive in a genuinely open, learning culture. I see this as a continuous learning cycle with the patient at the centre, with improvement being the aim at a micro and macro level and probably several levels in between. What I have in mind is shown below.

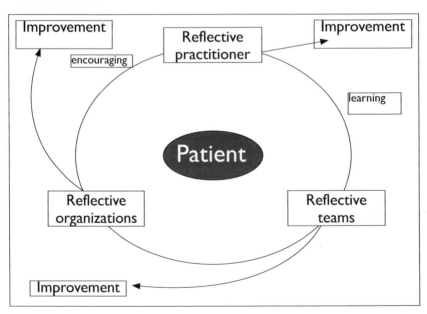

Figure 9.1 Switching on the Light

[See *Figure 9.1*. We thank Helen for allowing us to use her work.]

All this may sound like pretty heady stuff, and out of reach. It is, however, more than an abstract idea. It is the embryo of a vision for the future where reflection is embraced both in principle and in practice. Some healthcare organizations have embarked on this journey and are making good progress (Ghaye 2008). It is an expression of a 'better way'. It will not 'just happen', nor will it take place overnight. In the brief sketch of some of the attributes of a reflective organization above, we can see all the elements within this book beginning to come together. It moves us to a reconsideration of what we mean by 'whole person learning', team and organizational learning. We can see that within reflective organizations there is a clear meaning-making dimension in which, at every level, reflection gives meaning to and finds meaning in our caring work. There are valuing and feeling dimensions, confronting and structuring or reflections on context: Towards the reflective organization restructuring elements as well. It is a sketch of a kind of workplace for the 21st century.

Without a vision for tomorrow, hope is impossible.
(Freire 1998:.45)

References

Andersen T, ed. (1991) *The Reflecting Team: Dialogues and dialogues about the dialogues.* W W Norton and Company, New York

Argyris C (1999) *On Organizational Learning.* Blackwell Business, Oxford

Blanchard K et al (1999) *The Three Keys to Empowerment.* Berrett-Koehler Publishers, San Francisco

Eraut M (1995) *Developing professional knowledge within a client-centred orientation.* in Guskey T, Huberman M, eds Professional Development in Education: New Paradigms and Practices. Teachers College Press, New York

Freire P, Faundez A (1989) *Learning to Question: A Pedagogy of Liberation.* WCC Publications, Geneva

Freire P (1998) *Pedagogy of the Heart.* Continuum Press, New York

Fullan M (1999) *Change Forces: The Sequel.* The Falmer Press, London

Ghaye, T. (2008) *Building the Reflective Healthcare Organization.* Blackwell Publishing, Oxford.

Ghaye T, Gillespie D, Lillyman S, eds (2000) *Empowerment through Reflection: The narratives of healthcare professionals.* Mark Allen Publishing, Salisbury

Jack R, ed. (1995) *Empowerment in Community Care*. Macmillan Press, Basingstoke

Kendall S (1998) *Health and Empowerment: Research and practice*. Arnold Publishers, London

Senge P et al (1999) *The Dance of Change: The challenges of sustaining momentum in learning organizations*. Nicholas Brealey Publishing, London

Wright S, ed. (1998) *Changing Nursing Practice*. Arnold Publishers, London

CHAPTER 10

Behind the learning curve: Thinking again and thoughtful possibilities for practice

We need languages that regenerate us, warm us, give birth to us, that lead us to act and not to flee.
(Chawaf cited by Marks and Courtivron 1981: 43)

This has been a book about and for the enhancement of caring work through reflection. It has been a blend of principle with practice. Some of the ideas we have discussed will have been familiar to you. Others are perhaps new and challenging. We have deliberately written it in this way to try to create a powerful image in your mind of the educative potency of reflective practice. We have attempted to avoid using a language of division, for this has not helped healthcare to mature as a profession. We have tried to avoid exacerbating existing divisions which often show themselves in such language as 'theory-practice gap', 'high ground and swampy lowlands', 'practical or propositional knowledge', and instead have tried to show how reflective practice works with notions such as synthesis, interface and interaction. Above all else, we have made an attempt to join up the notion of the practice 'centredness' of healthcare with that of reflection-on-practice. We have endeavoured to create a synthesis between our caring work, those we care for and the way we learn about their interaction and transformation through reflective practice. We wish to argue that these things are the active ingredients of intelligent, informed, safe and accountable practice.

....we must ensure that our descriptions, our practice and our research present a united message; a message which fosters reflection.
(Lumby 1997: 481)

Writing this book has been a creative experience. In thinking again about what we have done, we believe we can claim that we have begun to create an emerging 'landscape of reflective practice' (*Figure 10.1*). It is

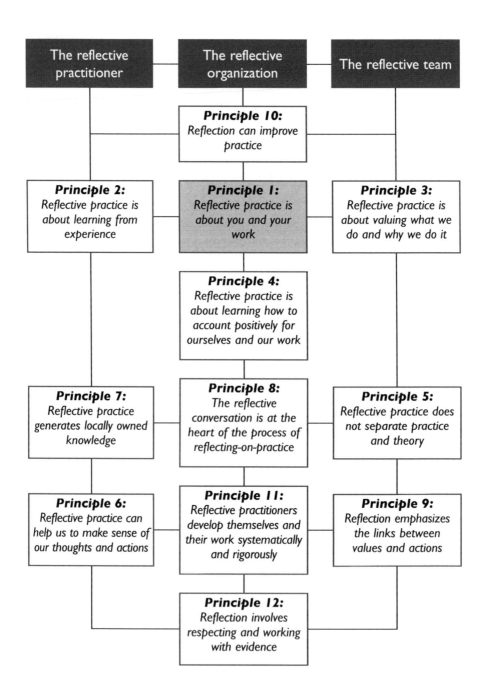

Figure 10.1 An emerging landscape of reflective practice
(Note: 1 to 12 are the principles of reflective practice presented in this book)

a landscape with some familiar landmarks, some things of interest, some hazardous and problematic features, some routes or links which help to make each landmark accessible and more understandable as we see one in relation to another.

Figure 10.1, then, is a kind of 'map' which you might like to use as you navigate your way around this emerging landscape. Having read the book you will no doubt appreciate that the landscape is far from being flat, featureless, boring and unchanging. Neither is it merely a landscape of 'high hard ground and murky, swampy lowlands' (Schön 1983). It is richly patterned and, in the foreground, in sharp focus and relief are the first three principles:

1. Reflective practice is about you and your work.
2. Reflective practice is about leaving from experience.
3. Reflective practice is about valuing what we do and why we do it.

In the middle distance, no less vivid or colourful are principles four to twelve. They are:

4. Reflective practice is about learning how to account positively for ourselves and our work.
5. Reflective practice does not separate practice and theory.
6. Reflective practice can help us make sense of our thoughts and actions.
7. Reflective practice generates locally owned knowledge.
8. The reflective conversation is at the heart of the process of reflecting-on-practice.
10. Reflection can improve practice.
11. Reflective practitioners develop themselves and their work systematically and rigorously.
12. Reflection involves respecting and working with evidence.

On the far horizon there is a new and possible world. It is one where individuals (reflective practitioners) begin to assemble and organize themselves into high performance groups (reflective teams). As we focus our gaze on this horizon we can see that, sometimes, these teams come together into an empowered collective (the reflective organization). The individual features of this emerging landscape of reflective practice are not unique. They are found elsewhere on other landscapes.

What makes the landscape of reflective practice special, interesting and worth experiencing, is the particular configuration, or the arrangement, of its individual features. It is a uniqueness which arises from a synthesis. When taken together, the individual features begin to help us to appreciate how reflective practice and reflective healthcare practitioners are potent parts of a joined up or 'connected profession', with the courage, clarity of thinking and sensitivities to take control over its own destiny. Perhaps such a bold claim is worth reflecting upon?

References

Lumby J (1997) *Threads of an emerging discipline: praxis, reflection, rhetoric and research.* In Gray G, Pratt R eds Towards a Discipline of Nursing. Churchill Livingstone, Melbourne.

Marks E, de Courtivron I (1981) *New French Feminisms.* Harvester Press Limited, Sussex

Schön D (1983) *The Reflective Practitioner.* Basic Books, New York

Index

A

action
  appreciative 11
  plan 120
  research 116, 120
action-reflection cycle 130
advocacy 92
appreciative
  action 11
  intent 9
  reflection
    framework for 12
authority 32

B

borrowing
  knowledge 33

C

caring 119
  values 71
chaos theory 50
clinical
  conversation
    analysis of 81
    qualities of 83
  decisions xv
  supervision 54
codes of conduct 106–108
concept mapping 122
connections
  between supervisor and supervisee 80
constructive challenge 74

continuing professional development
  (CPD) 105
conversation
  as part of oral enquiry 69
  clinical 68, 76–78
    analysis of 81
    qualities of 83
  collaborative 69
  purpose of 67–68
  reflective 67, 70–72
    qualities of 71
  serious 69
  triadic 85
  types of 69
critical incidence analysis 123

D

decision-making process xv–xvii
deficit trap 10
Dewey, John 46, 113
dialogue 73
dialogue, *see* conversation 68
diaries, *see* journal writing

E

educative practice 117
empowerment 75, 132
enlightenment 75
evidence-based practice 76

F

fuzzy
  logic 49
  thinking 49

H

Health Professional Council (HPC)
  standards of care 106
human communication
  complexity of 73

I

improvement process 115
incident analysis 123
intent, appreciative 9

J

journal writing 123

K

knowing-in-action 56–57
knowledge 130
  as authority 32
  borrowing 33
  factual 27
  outsider 29
  personal-practical 29, 30–31
  practical 53
  propositional 27
  questions 26
  theoretical 55, 62
  values-based 27

L

learning
  journal 123
  log 123
  work-based 6
lifelong learning 5
living theory 37–39

M

meta-reflection 56, 58
models 59
  cyclical 59
  flexible 59
  focused 59
  holistic 60

N

Nightingale, Florence 34

P

patterns 51
personal-practical knowledge 25, 77
personal growth 47
practitioner-researcher
  reflective 118
problem solving 7

Q

quality improvement 6
questions 72
  reflective 130

R

reflection xiv
  appreciative 1–12, 7–10
    framework for 12
  gap 129
  in action 3
  on being professional 89–102
  on experience 25–42
  principles of 138
  productive 5
  role in improving practice 114
  types related to concerns and contexts
    61
reflection-action-reflection
  cycle 130
reflection-in-action 56–57
reflection-on-practice xv–xviii, 56, 58,
    79–80
reflective
  clinical conversation 76–77
  conversation xiv, 67, 70–72
    qualities of 71
  cycles 2
  learning cycle 2
  spirals 2
  practice
    map 138
  practice example 15–22